Elements in Quantitative Finance
edited by
Riccardo Rebonato
EDHEC Business School

GIRSANOV, NUMERAIRES, AND ALL THAT

Patrick S. Hagan
Gorilla Science

Andrew Lesniewski
Baruch College

Shaftesbury Road, Cambridge CB2 8EA, United Kingdom

One Liberty Plaza, 20th Floor, New York, NY 10006, USA

477 Williamstown Road, Port Melbourne, VIC 3207, Australia

314–321, 3rd Floor, Plot 3, Splendor Forum, Jasola District Centre, New Delhi – 110025, India

103 Penang Road, #05–06/07, Visioncrest Commercial, Singapore 238467

Cambridge University Press is part of Cambridge University Press & Assessment, a department of the University of Cambridge.

We share the University's mission to contribute to society through the pursuit of education, learning and research at the highest international levels of excellence.

www.cambridge.org
Information on this title: www.cambridge.org/9781009339285
DOI: 10.1017/9781009339278

First published 2022

A catalogue record for this publication is available from the British Library.

ISBN 978-1-009-33928-5 Paperback
ISSN 2631-8571 (online)
ISSN 2631-8563 (print)

Girsanov, Numeraires, and All That

Elements in Quantitative Finance

DOI: 10.1017/9781009339278
First published online: October 2022

Patrick S. Hagan
Gorilla Science
Andrew Lesniewski
Baruch College

Author for correspondence: Andrew Lesniewski,
Andrew.Lesniewski@baruch.cuny.edu

Abstract: In this Element, the authors review the technique of the change of numeraire in the martingale approach to option pricing. Their intention is to present a reader-friendly explanation of the technique itself, and illustrate how it is applied in various fields of quantitative finance as the basis for building option valuation models. They start with an informal review of Girsanov's theorem, followed by a brief summary of the basic concepts of the arbitrage free pricing, and the technique of change of numeraire. This is followed by a number of applications of the change of numeraire technique including interest rate models, FX quanto adjustments, credit risk modeling, mortgage-backed securities, and CMS rates.

Keywords: Girsanov's theorem, change of measure, numeraire, martingale pricing, financial derivatives

ISBNs: 9781009339285 (PB), 9781009339278 (OC)
ISSNs: 2631-8571 (online), 2631-8563 (print)

Contents

1 Introduction

This Element is a pedagogical introduction to the technique of the change of numeraire in the martingale approach to option pricing, also known as arbitrage free pricing theory. Our intention is to present a reader-friendly explanation of the technique itself, and illustrate how it is applied in various fields of quantitative finance as the basis for building option valuation models. These applications include interest rate modeling, credit risk modeling, foreign exchange modeling, and others. We do not aspire to present an exhaustive list of such applications, or all the details of the markets, financial instruments, and models where martingale methods are particularly effective. Instead, we hope to provide the reader with enough background to be able to use the technique in his or her work.

The central concept of arbitrage free pricing is that of a *numeraire*. From the economic point of view, a numeraire is a tradeable asset conventionally used to quote prices of other tradeable goods. For example, currently most international commodities are traded using the US dollar as the numeraire. Historically, many other assets have been used as numeraires, such as certain metals (bronze, gold, silver), salt, agricultural products, and others. The choice of numeraire is dictated by convenience, and there is equivalence of asset prices expressed in terms of different numeraires. From the financial engineering perspective, a numeraire is a useful technical device that allows us to express certain financial transactions in conceptually transparent terms, and model their price processes as martingales. This point of view was first proposed in [10].

The key mathematical result that underlies this mechanism is *Girsanov's theorem*, which relates the change of the drift coefficient in an Ito process to a "change of variables" in the underlying probability measure. What is now known as Girsanov's theorem is actually a culmination of efforts by a number of mathematicians (notably Cameron, Martin, and Girsanov), who studied the effect of a change of variables in the measure on a probability space associated with a Brownian motion on the properties of a stochastic process on this space. It gives an explicit expression for the Radon–Nikodym derivative of such a change of variables in terms of the parameters of the stochastic process. A thorough and, at the same time, accessible mathematical presentation of stochastic calculus is presented in [21].

Girsanov's theorem plays a key conceptual role in arbitrage free pricing theory, which is the basis for the classical approach to derivatives pricing theory. The key tenet of this theory is *lack of arbitrage* (i.e. the inability to design portfolio strategies that generate riskless profit). Within this framework, lack of arbitrage opportunities is essentially equivalent to the ability of modeling asset prices as martingales. And while it is debatable whether the actual financial markets do not present arbitrage opportunities, arbitrage free pricing leads to a robust conceptual framework for derivatives modeling.

This Element is organized as follows. We start with an informal review of Girsanov's theorem, which is at the core of the arguments presented in the Element. This is followed by a brief review of the basic concepts of the arbitrage free pricing, just enough to cover our needs. We discuss the probabilistic concepts underlying this framework, but we do not delve into the nontrivial technical issues while doing so. For a full account of this theory, we refer to the original papers [15] and [16], as well as the thorough textbook presentation in [2] and [20]. Next, we discuss the technique of change of numeraire and derive the fundamental explicit relation between the drift coefficients corresponding to the same diffusion process under two different numeraires. This is followed by a number of important applications of the change of numeraire technique in interest rate models, FX quanto adjustments, credit risk modeling, mortgage-backed securities, and constant maturity swap (CMS) rates.

The intended style of exposition of the Element is conversational. We do not strive for mathematical rigor, using instead the "physics level" of mathematical reasoning. The theorems we quote do not always provide complete lists of technical assumptions, but focus instead on their financial relevance. On the finance side, we make technical simplifications as well. In the descriptions of fixed income instruments, we neglect various details, such as the delay between rate fixing dates and contract settlement dates, detailed definitions of the relevant day count fractions, business day conventions, precise conventions regarding various settlement days, and so on. In order to focus the discussion on the central concepts and not to obscure it with details, we also disregard the presence of some "bases" between various rates. Capturing these bases by mathematical models often presents mathematical challenges of their own.

2 Girsanov's Theorem

Before we move to finance, we start by reviewing the main mathematical result underlying much of formalism that follows, namely Girsanov's theorem.

The toy version of Girsanov's theorem is the following elementary calculation involving two Gaussian probability measures (or distributions) on the real axis. Consider two such measures:

$$d\mathsf{P}(x) = \frac{1}{\sqrt{2\pi}\sigma} \exp\Big(-\frac{(x-\mu)^2}{2\sigma^2}\Big)dx, \tag{1}$$

and

$$dQ(x) = \frac{1}{\sqrt{2\pi}\sigma} \exp\Big(-\frac{(x-\nu)^2}{2\sigma^2}\Big)dx. \tag{2}$$

Note that P and Q may have different means, but they share the same variance. Then, manipulating the quadratic function in the exponential, we find that the following relation holds:

$$dQ(x) = L(x)dP(x), \tag{3}$$

where

$$L(x) = \exp\Big(\frac{(\nu-\mu)(x-\mu)}{\sigma^2} - \frac{1}{2}\frac{(\nu-\mu)^2}{\sigma^2}\Big). \tag{4}$$

Clearly,

$$\int_{-\infty}^{\infty} L(x)dP(x) = 1. \tag{5}$$

The function $L(x)$ is positive for all x and can suggestively be written as the "derivative" of measure Q with respect to measure P,

$$L(x) = \frac{dQ}{dP}(x), \tag{6}$$

known as the Radon–Nikodym derivative. One can think about the Radon–Nikodym derivative as an extension of the concept of the Jacobian of a change of variables familiar from calculus.

2.1 Radon–Nikodym Derivative

We now consider a one-dimensional Brownian motion $W(t)$. Let the associated *probability space* be denoted by $(\Omega, \mathcal{F}, P)$, where Ω is the sample space, $\mathcal{F} = (\mathcal{F}_t)_{t\geq 0}$ is the filtered information set, and P is the probability measure. A sample $\omega \in \Omega$ is a realization (that is, a possible trajectory) of the Brownian motion, that is, a continuous function $\omega(t), t \geq 0$, with $\omega(0) = 0$. All possible sample paths up to time $t > 0$ form the information set $\mathcal{F}_t$, which represents the history of the process known at the time t.

The probability measure P is a Gaussian measure defined so that the following two conditions hold. For any $s < t$, the increment $\Delta W(s,t) = W(t) - W(s)$ has expected value 0,

$$E[\Delta W(s,t)] = 0, \tag{7}$$

and variance equal to the time increment:

$$E[\Delta W(s,t)^2] = t - s. \tag{8}$$

Furthermore, any two such increments $\Delta W(s_1, t_1)$ and $\Delta W(s_2, t_2)$, with $t_1 < s_2$, are assumed independent:

$$\mathsf{E}[\Delta W(s_1, t_1)\Delta W(s_2, t_2)] = 0. \tag{9}$$

In other words, a Brownian motion advances by an amount ΔW over time Δt according to the Gaussian probability distribution (1) with $\mu = 0$ and $\sigma = \sqrt{\Delta t}$.

By $\mathsf{E}[X] = \int_\Omega X(\omega)dP(\omega)$ (or $\mathsf{E}^P[X]$, whenever we want to be precise about the probability measure) we denote the expected value of a random variable X with respect to the measure P. We will also be concerned with the conditional expected value $\mathsf{E}[X|\mathscr{F}_t]$ of X given the information available up to time t. Interchangeably, whenever we want to save space, we will be denoting this quantity by $\mathsf{E}_t[X]$.

Consider now two probability measures P and Q on an abstract (not necessarily associated with a Brownian motion) probability space Ω. We say that Q is *absolutely continuous* with respect to P if probability zero events with respect to P are also probability zero under Q, that is, if it satisfies the following condition:

$$\text{for a set } A \subset \Omega, \text{ if } \mathsf{P}(A) = 0, \text{ then also } \mathsf{Q}(A) = 0. \tag{10}$$

An important classic theorem of real analysis states that if Q is absolutely continuous with respect to P, then there exists a positive function $L(\omega)$ on Ω, called the *Radon–Nikodym derivative*, or the *likelihood ratio*, such that $L(\omega)$ is integrable with respect to P, and

$$\mathsf{Q}(A) = \int_A L(\omega)d\mathsf{P}(\omega), \tag{11}$$

for all $A \subset \Omega$. In particular,

$$\int_\Omega L(\omega)d\mathsf{P}(\omega) = 1. \tag{12}$$

In general, not much more about L is known other than it exists. A quick and clever proof of this theorem, due to von Neumann, is presented in [25].

One can express relation (11) suggestively as

$$\frac{d\mathsf{Q}}{d\mathsf{P}}(\omega) = L(\omega). \tag{13}$$

In other words, the "volume element" $d\mathsf{Q}$ is always proportional to the "volume element" $d\mathsf{P}$, with the proportionality factor that is a positive function throughout the probability space.

Two probability measures Q and P are called *equivalent*, if Q is absolutely continuous with respect to P and P is absolutely continuous with respect to Q. This means that these two measures have exactly the same sets of measure zero (and, consequently, the same sets of measure one).

In the context of a Brownian motion, we can encode the dependence of the Radon–Nikodym derivative on the filtration by time. Namely, we consider the conditional expected value

$$L(\omega, t) = \mathsf{E}_t[L(\omega)], \tag{14}$$

which represents the knowledge of $L(\omega)$ based on the information available at time t. In the following, we will be suppressing the dependence of $L(\omega, t)$ on ω, and denote it simply by $L(t)$. In other words, $L(t)$ is a stochastic process.

2.2 Girsanov's Theorem in One Dimension

Consider now a *diffusion process* $X(t)$ defined by the following stochastic differential equation (SDE) in the sense of Ito:

$$dX(t) = \mu(X(t), t)dt + c(X(t), t)dW(t), \tag{15}$$

which starts at some initial value X_0. The coefficients $\mu(X(t), t)$ and $c(X(t), t)$ in (15) are called the *drift* and *diffusion* coefficients, respectively. A convenient way of thinking about a diffusion process is in terms of discretizing it over finite time increments and following sequentially each sample path through a Monte Carlo simulation. In this picture, $\mu(X(t), t)$ is the local mean of a Gaussian distribution, while $c(X(t), t)$ is the local standard deviation of that distribution.

In the light of the toy calculation in the beginning of this section, a natural question then arises: can we transform a diffusion process into a diffusion process with a different drift,

$$dX(t) = \widetilde{\mu}(X(t), t)dt + c(X(t), t)d\widetilde{W}(t), \tag{16}$$

by a change to an equivalent probability measure Q? In particular, can we make the new process a martingale?

Recall that a process $X(t)$ is a *martingale* if $\mathsf{E}^{\mathsf{Q}}\left[|X(t)|\right] < \infty$, for all t, and

$$X(s) = \mathsf{E}^{\mathsf{Q}}\left[X(t)|\mathscr{F}_s\right], \tag{17}$$

where $\mathsf{E}^{\mathsf{Q}}\left[\,\cdot\,|\mathscr{F}_s\right]$ denotes conditional expected value. In other words, given all information up to time s, the expected value of any future value of a martingale is the current value $X(s)$. The diffusion process $X(t)$ is a martingale, if the diffusion here is driftless (i.e. $\widetilde{\mu}(X(t), t) = 0$).

An affirmative answer to this question is provided by Girsanov's theorem. One might heuristically proceed like this. Write

$$\begin{aligned} dX(t) &= \widetilde{\mu}(X(t), t)dt + c(X(t), t)\Big(\frac{\mu(X(t), t) - \widetilde{\mu}(X(t), t)}{c(X(t), t)}\, dt + dW(t)\Big) \\ &= \widetilde{\mu}(X(t), t)dt + c(X(t), t)d\widetilde{W}(t), \end{aligned}$$

where

$$\widetilde{W}(t) = W(t) + \int_0^t \frac{\mu(X(s),s) - \widetilde{\mu}(X(s),s)}{c(X(s),s)}\, ds$$
$$\equiv W(t) - \int_0^t \theta(s)\, ds, \tag{18}$$

and we would like to interpret $\widetilde{W}(t)$ as a new Brownian motion. The presence of the shift $\int_0^t \theta(s)ds$ creates, however, an issue, as it leads to violation of conditions (7) and (9). The calculation at the beginning of this section suggests that this can be remedied by changing to a different, but equivalent, probability measure.

Girsanov's theorem asserts that indeed, under some technical assumptions on the drift and diffusion coefficients, $\widetilde{W}(t)$ defined in (18) is a Brownian motion, provided that the probability measure is modified appropriately.

More specifically, let us define the positive stochastic process:

$$L(t) = \exp\Big(\int_0^t \theta(s)\, dW(s) - \frac{1}{2}\int_0^t \theta(s)^2 ds\Big). \tag{19}$$

Recall that since L is a stochastic process, we have suppressed its explicit dependence on ω. We now define the equivalent measure Q by the requirement that its Radon–Nikodym derivative with respect to P is given by

$$\frac{d\mathsf{Q}}{d\mathsf{P}}(t) = L(t). \tag{20}$$

Let us emphasize that the Radon–Nikodym derivative $L(t)$ has an explicit form, built out of the data that define the process $X(t)$.

THEOREM (Girsanov's theorem). *Assume that the following technical condition (Novikov's condition) holds:*

$$\mathsf{E}^{\mathsf{P}}\Big[\exp\Big(\frac{1}{2}\int_0^t \theta(s)^2 ds\Big)\Big] < \infty. \tag{21}$$

Then:

(i) The process $L(t)$ is a martingale under P. Furthermore, it satisfies the following stochastic differential equation:

$$dL(t) = L(t)\theta(t)dW(t). \tag{22}$$

(ii) The process $\widetilde{W}(t)$ is a Brownian motion under Q.

2.3 Girsanov's Theorem in Many Dimensions

We have stated Girsanov's theorem for the case of a one-dimensional Brownian motion. This assumption is not really essential and, using a bit of linear algebra, one can easily formulate a version of Girsanov's theorem for an arbitrary multidimensional Brownian motion.

Consider an n-dimensional Brownian motion $W(t) = (W_1(t), \ldots, W_n(t))$, whose components are uncorrelated one-dimensional Brownian motions,

$$dW_i(t)dW_j(t) = 0, \text{ for } i \neq j.$$

This assumption is not a real loss of generality: if we work with an n-dimensional Brownian motion whose components are correlated with a constant correlation matrix ρ,

$$dW_i(t)dW_j(t) = \rho_{ij}dt, \text{ for } i \neq j,$$

then we decompose each $W_j(t)$ in terms of the independent components and redefine the diffusion coefficients appropriately. Consider an n-dimensional diffusion process $X(t) = (X_1(t), \ldots, X_n(t))$, given by the system of SDEs:

$$dX(t) = \mu(X(t), t)dt + c(X(t), t)dW(t), \tag{23}$$

where the drift $\mu(X(t), t)$ is a vector that takes values in $\mathbb{R}^n$, and the $n \times n$ matrix of diffusion coefficients $c(X(t), t)$ is assumed to be nonsingular.

Now, define the stochastic process:

$$L(t) = \exp\Big(\int_0^t \theta(s)^{\mathrm{T}}\, dW(s) - \frac{1}{2}\int_0^t \theta(s)^{\mathrm{T}}\theta(s)ds\Big), \tag{24}$$

where

$$\theta(t) = c(X(t), t)^{-1}\big(\widetilde{\mu}(X(t), t) - \mu(X(t), t)\big), \tag{25}$$

and where ^{T} denotes transpose. Let $\widetilde{W}(t)$ be the shifted vector-valued Brownian motion:

$$\widetilde{W}(t) = W(t) - \int_0^t \theta(s)\, ds. \tag{26}$$

THEOREM (Girsanov's theorem – multidimensional version). *Assume that the following technical condition (Novikov's condition) holds:*

$$\mathsf{E}^{\mathsf{P}}\Big[\exp\Big(\frac{1}{2}\int_0^t \theta(s)^{\mathrm{T}}\theta(s)ds\Big)\Big] < \infty. \tag{27}$$

Then:

(i) The process $L(t)$ is a martingale under P. *Furthermore, it satisfies the following stochastic differential equation:*

$$dL(t) = L(t)\theta(t)^{\mathrm{T}}dW(t). \tag{28}$$

(ii) The process $\widetilde{W}(t)$ is a Brownian motion under Q.

3 Arbitrage Asset Pricing in a Nutshell

3.1 Frictionless Market Models

We consider a model of a *frictionless* financial market that consists of n (risky) assets $I_1, \ldots, I_n$. By frictionless we mean that:

(i) each of the assets is *liquid* (i.e. at each time any bid or ask order, regardless of size, can be immediately executed),
(ii) there are no *transaction costs* (i.e. each bid and ask order for each security at time t is executed at the same price level and without a commission),
(iii) executing an order, regardless of its size, leaves no *impact* on the market,
(iv) there is no *counterparty risk* (i.e. market participants do not default on fulfilling the terms of a trade).

This is obviously a gross oversimplification of reality, and much work has been done to relax these assumptions. From the conceptual point of view, however, it leads to a profound and workable framework of asset pricing theory. This is very much like the formulation of Newtonian gravity in vacuum, which neglects friction and energy dissipation.

We model the price processes of these assets by a vector of continuous time stochastic processes $S(t) = (S_1(t), \ldots, S_n(t))$, where $S_i(t)$ denotes the price process of asset I_i at time t. We emphasize that these processes represent market observable asset prices, and not merely some convenient state variables. We assume that each price process is a diffusion process. In other words, there is an underlying probability space $(\Omega, (\mathscr{F}_t)_{t\geq 0}, \mathrm{P})$ generated by a multidimensional Brownian motion $W(t) = (W_1(t), \ldots, W_d(t))$, which drives the price process,

$$dS(t) = \mu(S(t), t)dt + c(S(t), t)dW(t). \tag{29}$$

Here $\mu = (\mu_1, \ldots, \mu_n)$ and $c = (c_{ij})_{1\leq i\leq n, 1\leq j\leq d}$ are the vector of drift coefficients and the matrix of diffusion coefficients, respectively.

In order to develop an intuition for the concepts explained below, we recall the basic example from the world of equity derivatives.

EXAMPLE (Black–Scholes model). In this classic model of equity derivatives, $S_1(t) = B(t)$ is the riskless money market account, and $S_2(t) = S(t)$ is a risky stock, with the dynamics given by

$$\begin{aligned} dB(t) &= rB(t)dt, \\ dS(t) &= \mu S(t)dt + \sigma S(t)dW(t). \end{aligned} \tag{30}$$

The rate of return r on the money market account is called the *riskless rate*, while μ is the rate of return on the risky asset. The financial reality is that there is no such thing as riskless rate (whose closest proxy, in the US dollar market, is the SOFR rate), but its presence in the Black–Scholes model helps one understand the general framework of risk neutral valuation.

3.2 Self-Financing Portfolios and No Arbitrage

A *portfolio* is specified by the vector of weights $w(t) = (w_1(t), \ldots, w_n(t))$, according to which capital is allocated to each asset at time t. We assume that $w(t)$ is a process adapted to the information set $\mathscr{F}_t$. In other words, all allocation decisions in the portfolio are made based on the information available up to time t. We also assume that the weights are nonnegative, and they add up to one.

The value process of the portfolio is given by

$$V(t) = w(t)^{\mathrm{T}} S(t). \tag{31}$$

A portfolio is *self-financing*, if

$$dV(t) = w(t)^{\mathrm{T}} dS(t), \tag{32}$$

or, equivalently,

$$V(t) = V(0) + \int_0^t w(s)^{\mathrm{T}} dS(s). \tag{33}$$

In other words, the price process of a self-financing portfolio does not allow for infusion or withdrawal of capital. It is entirely driven by price processes of the constituent instruments and their weights.

A fundamental assumption of arbitrage pricing theory is that financial markets (or at least, their models) are free of arbitrage opportunities.[1] An *arbitrage opportunity* arises if one can construct a self-financing portfolio such that:

(i) the initial value of the portfolio is zero, $V(0) = 0$,
(ii) with probability one, the portfolio has a nonnegative value at maturity, $\mathsf{P}(V(T) \geq 0) = 1$,
(iii) with a positive probability, the value of the portfolio at maturity is positive, $\mathsf{P}(V(T) > 0) > 0$.

[1] This assumption is, mercifully, violated frequently enough so that much of the financial industry can sustain itself exploiting the market's lack of respect for arbitrage freeness.

We say the model is *arbitrage free* if it does not allow arbitrage opportunities. As we shall see in the next section, requiring arbitrage freeness has important consequences for price dynamics.

3.3 Complete Markets

A random variable X on the probability space $(\Omega, (\mathscr{F}_t)_{t\geq 0}, \mathsf{P})$ is square integrable if $\mathsf{E}[X^2] < \infty$. In other words, a square integrable random variable has a well-defined variance. A financial market is called *complete* if each such random variable can be obtained as the terminal value of a self-financing trading strategy, that is, if there exists a self-financing portfolio such that $X = V(T)$.

This somewhat technical sounding condition has a natural interpretation. If we think about X as the price of a (possibly very complicated) contingent claim, market completeness means that such a claim can be replicated by way of a self-financing trading strategy. In practical terms it means that the price of a contingent claim is uniquely determined in terms of the replicating portfolio. Completeness is a convenient but restrictive assumption, and many widely used models violate it. We will discuss some of such models in what follows.

EXAMPLE (Black–Scholes model revisited). To illustrate this concept, we consider again the Black–Scholes model. Let $g(S(T))$ be a time T payoff. For example, $g(S(T)) = \max(S(T) - K, 0)$ corresponds to a call option struck at K. Let $v = v(x,t)$ be the solution to the terminal value problem:

$$\begin{aligned} \frac{\partial \varphi}{\partial t} + rx\frac{\partial v}{\partial x} + \frac{1}{2}\sigma^2 x^2 \frac{\partial^2 v}{\partial x^2} - rv = 0, \\ v(x,t) = g(x). \end{aligned} \tag{34}$$

This is the terminal value problem for the Black–Scholes (or backward Kolmogorov) equation arising in the Black–Scholes model, and which is a consequence of Ito's lemma. Then, the portfolio with weights

$$\begin{aligned} w_1(t) &= \frac{v(S(t),t) - S(t)\frac{\partial v(S(t),t)}{\partial x}}{B(t)}, \\ w_2(t) &= \frac{\partial v(S(t),t)}{\partial x} \end{aligned} \tag{35}$$

is the replicating portfolio for the payoff $g(S(T))$. Indeed, $w_2(t)$ is the option delta, which is the dynamically updated number of shares of the underlying asset, and $w_1(t)$ is the number of units of the riskless bond. The value of this portfolio is, as expected, equal to

$$V(t) = v(S(t),t). \tag{36}$$

Multi-asset markets of the form (29) are, in general, not complete. Verifying that a market model is complete in the strict mathematical sense is usually very hard, but also not really necessary from a practical perspective. A useful rule of thumb is that a multi-asset market (29) is complete, if and only if

(i) $n = d$ (i.e. the number of assets equals the number of stochastic factors), and
(ii) the matrix $\sigma(S(t), t)$ is invertible for all $t \leq T$ with probability 1 (some more technical conditions may be required).

3.4 The Fundamental Theorems of Arbitrage Pricing

A key concept in modern asset pricing theory is that of a *numeraire*. Mathematically, a numeraire is any *tradeable* asset with price process $N(t)$, such that $N(t) > 0$, for all times t. It is always tacitly assumed that asset prices are expressed in terms of the relevant currency as numeraire. This can be the local currency of the financial market, or it can be a global currency, such as the US dollar, in case of markets (such as the crude oil markets) whose economics require it. For financial modeling purposes, it is often convenient to allow other assets $N(t)$ as numeraires. The *relative price* process of asset I_i is defined by

$$S_i^N(t) = \frac{S_i(t)}{N(t)} . \tag{37}$$

In other words, the relative price of an asset is its price expressed in the units of the numeraire rather than in currency units.

A probability measure Q is called an *equivalent martingale measure* (EMM) for a financial market model, associated with numeraire $N(t)$, if it has the following properties:

(a) Q is equivalent to P, that is,

$$dP = L_{PQ}\, dQ,$$

and

$$dQ = L_{QP}\, dP,$$

with likelihood ratios $L_{PQ} > 0$ and $L_{QP} > 0$.

(b) The relative price processes $S_i^N(t)$ are martingales under Q,

$$S_i^N(s) = \mathsf{E}^{Q}\left[S_i^N(t)\middle|\mathcal{F}_s\right] . \tag{38}$$

The existence of an EMM allows thus, at least in principle, to transform an arbitrary stochastic price dynamics into a martingale dynamics. The advantage of doing so may be conceptual clarity of the model, and the model may also be analytically and computationally more tractable.

The fact that such a transformation is possible for arbitrage free market models is a cornerstone of arbitrage pricing theory. It is expressed in the two fundamental theorems of arbitrage pricing, which follow. The first of these theorems guarantees the existence of an EMM.

THEOREM (First Fundamental Theorem of Arbitrage Pricing). *A market is arbitrage free if and only if for each numeraire there exists an equivalent martingale measure* Q.

In other words, arbitrage freeness of a model means the existence, given a numeraire $N(t)$, of an equivalent measure such that the relative price process is a martingale under this measure. In practical terms, in an arbitrage free market, we can redefine the Brownian motion so that the prices of all assets in the units of the numeraire are given by driftless SDEs.

This theorem is formulated in a somewhat cavalier way, as we have disregarded some important technical assumptions, and it should be thought of as a metatheorem. Its precise formulation and proof are quite technical, and is outside the scope of this Element. However, we shall indicate how the existence of an EMM implies lack of arbitrage.

Let N be a numeraire, and let Q be a measure under which all S_i^Ns are martingales. We first verify that a self-financing portfolio, when expressed in terms of the relative prices S_i^N, is self-financing, that is,

$$dV^N(t) = w(t)^{\mathrm{T}} dS^N(t).$$

Indeed, using Ito's lemma,

$$\begin{aligned} dV^N(t) &= d\left(\frac{V(t)}{N(t)}\right) \\ &= \frac{dV(t)}{N(t)} - \frac{V(t)dN(t)}{N(t)^2} - \frac{dV(t)dN(t)}{N(t)^2} \\ &= w(t)^{\mathrm{T}}\left(\frac{dS(t)}{N(t)} - \frac{S(t)dN(t)}{N(t)^2} - \frac{dS(t)dN(t)}{N(t)^2}\right) \\ &= w(t)^{\mathrm{T}} d\left(\frac{S(t)}{N(t)}\right) \\ &= w(t)^{\mathrm{T}} dS(t), \end{aligned}$$

as claimed.

Now, since all S_i^Ns are martingales, $S^N(t)$ is driftless, that is,

$$dS^N(t) = c(t)dW(t).$$

As a consequence, there is no drift term in $dV^N(t)$, and so $V^N(t)$ is a martingale. Since the measures P and Q are equivalent,

$$\begin{aligned} &\mathsf{Q}(V^N(T) > 0) > 0, \\ &\mathsf{Q}(V^N(T) \geq 0) = 1. \end{aligned}$$

Therefore,

$$\begin{aligned} V^N(0) &= \mathsf{E}^{\mathsf{Q}}[V^N(T)] \\ &> 0, \end{aligned}$$

which contradicts the assumption that the initial value of the portfolio is zero.

EXAMPLE (Black–Scholes model revisited). Consider again the Black–Scholes model. First, we choose the money market account as the numeraire,

$$\begin{aligned} N(t) &= B(t) \\ &= e^{rt}. \end{aligned}$$

With this choice of numeraire,

$$dS^B(t) = (\mu - r)S^B(t)dt + \sigma S^B(t)dW(t),$$

where $S^B(t)$ denotes the relative price process,

$$\begin{aligned} S^B(t) &= \frac{S(t)}{B(t)} \\ &= e^{-rt}S(t). \end{aligned}$$

Next, we use Girsanov's theorem in order to change the probability measure so that the relative price process is driftless,

$$dS^B(t) = \sigma S^B(t)dW(t).$$

Explicitly, this amounts to the following change of measure,

$$\frac{d\mathsf{Q}}{d\mathsf{P}}(t) = \exp\left(- \lambda W(t) - \frac{1}{2}\lambda^2 t \right),$$

where the ratio

$$\lambda = \frac{\mu - r}{\sigma}$$

is known as the *market price of risk.*

The second theorem links the uniqueness of the equivalent martingale measure to the concept of a complete market.

THEOREM (Second Fundamental Theorem of Arbitrage Pricing). *An arbitrage free market is complete if and only if, for each numeraire $N(t)$, the equivalent martingale measure Q is unique.*

In other words, in a complete, arbitrage free market, one and only one martingale measure Q corresponds to a given numeraire $N(t)$. For example, in the Black–Scholes model, the EMM we have constructed, is unique.

An important consequence of the Second Fundamental Theorem is the arbitrage pricing law:

$$\frac{V(s)}{N(s)} = \mathsf{E}^{\mathsf{Q}}\Big[\frac{V(t)}{N(t)}\,|\mathscr{F}_s\Big], \tag{39}$$

for all $s < t$. In particular,

$$V(0) = N(0)\,\mathsf{E}^{\mathsf{Q}}\Big[\frac{V(t)}{N(t)}\Big]. \tag{40}$$

3.5 Changing Numeraire

One is, of course, free to use another numeraire $M(t)$ instead of $N(t)$. Girsanov's theorem implies that there exists a martingale measure Q′ such that

$$\frac{V(s)}{M(s)} = \mathsf{E}^{\mathsf{Q}'}\Big[\frac{V(t)}{M(t)}\,|\mathscr{F}_s\Big]. \tag{41}$$

The Radon–Nikodym derivative is thus given by the ratio of the numeraires:

$$\begin{aligned}\frac{d\mathsf{Q}'}{d\mathsf{Q}}(t) &= \frac{\dfrac{N(0)}{N(t)}}{\dfrac{M(0)}{M(t)}}\\ &= \frac{N(0)}{M(0)}\,\frac{M(t)}{N(t)}\,.\end{aligned} \tag{42}$$

The choice of numeraire and the corresponding martingale measure is very much a matter of convenience, and is motivated by the problem at hand. We will see how this important technique works in practice. But before, we will derive an explicit formula for the change in the drift of a diffusion process under the change of the numeraire.

3.6 Drift Transformation under Change of Numeraire

Consider a complete financial market model as defined in Section 3. Suppose that we are interested in the dynamics of a n-dimensional state variable $X(t)$, whose components are not necessarily the price processes of tradeable assets. Under the measure P, its dynamics reads:

$$dX(t) = \mu_X^{\mathsf{P}}(t)dt + c_X(t)dW^{\mathsf{P}}(t). \tag{43}$$

In order to streamline the notation, we suppress the dependence of the coefficients in this equation (and the equations that follow) on the state variables (i.e. $\mu_X^{\mathsf{P}}(t) = \mu_X^{\mathsf{P}}(X(t), t)$, etc). Our goal is to relate this dynamics to the dynamics of the same state variable under an equivalent measure Q:

$$dX(t) = \mu_X^{\mathsf{Q}}(t)dt + c_X(t)dW_X^{\mathsf{Q}}(t). \tag{44}$$

Remember that the diffusion coefficients in these equations are unaffected by the change of measure! We assume that P is associated with the numeraire $N(t)$ whose dynamics is given by:

$$dN(t) = \mu_N(t)dt + c_N(t)dW^{\mathsf{P}}(t), \tag{45}$$

where $\mu_N(t)$ is a scalar, and $c_N(t)$ is a $1 \times n$ matrix, which can be thought of as a row vector. Similarly, Q is associated with the numeraire $M(t)$ whose dynamics under the P measure is given by:

$$dM(t) = \mu_M(t)dt + c_M(t)dW^{\mathsf{P}}(t). \tag{46}$$

According to Girsanov's theorem, the likelihood process $L(t)$ accompanying this change of measure is a martingale under the measure P, which satisfies the stochastic differential equation:

$$dL(t) = L(t)\theta(t)dW^{\mathsf{P}}(t), \tag{47}$$

with

$$\theta(t) = c_X(t)^{-1}\left(\mu_X^{\mathsf{Q}}(t) - \mu_X^{\mathsf{P}}(t)\right). \tag{48}$$

Explicitly, the likelihood process $L(t)$ is given by the stochastic exponential of the martingale $\int_0^t \theta(s)dW^{\mathsf{P}}(s)$:

$$L(t) = \exp\left(\int_0^t \theta(s)^{\mathrm{T}} dW^{\mathsf{P}}(s) - \frac{1}{2}\int_0^t \theta(s)^{\mathrm{T}}\theta(s)ds\right). \tag{49}$$

On the other hand, from (42),

$$L(t) = \frac{N(0)}{M(0)}\frac{M(t)}{N(t)}. \tag{50}$$

Since $L(t)$ is a martingale under P, we conclude that the process $M(t)/N(t)$ is driftless under P. The diffusion coefficient can be easily computed from Ito's lemma (we can disregard the terms proportional to dt, since, whatever they are, they are bound to cancel out against each other), and we find that

$$d\Big(\frac{N(0)}{M(0)}\frac{M(t)}{N(t)}\Big)=\frac{N(0)}{M(0)}\frac{M(t)}{N(t)}\Big(\frac{c_M(t)}{M(t)}-\frac{c_N(t)}{N(t)}\Big)dW^{\mathsf{P}}(t).$$

Comparing this with (47), we infer that

$$\theta(t)=\frac{c_M(t)^{\mathrm{T}}}{M(t)}-\frac{c_N(t)^{\mathrm{T}}}{N(t)}. \tag{51}$$

Using (48), we conclude that the change of the drift accompanying a change of numeraire is given by

$$\mu_X^{\mathsf{Q}}(t)-\mu_X^{\mathsf{P}}(t)=c_X(t)\Big(\frac{c_M(t)^{\mathrm{T}}}{M(t)}-\frac{c_N(t)^{\mathrm{T}}}{N(t)}\Big). \tag{52}$$

We can express equation (52) in a more intrinsic form. Recall that if $X(t)$ and $Y(t)$ are scalar diffusion processes, then their *covariation process* $\langle X,Y\rangle(t)$ is defined as

$$\begin{aligned}\langle X,Y\rangle(t)&=\int_0^t dX(s)^{\mathrm{T}}dY(s)\\&=\int_0^t c_X(s)^{\mathrm{T}}c_Y(s)ds.\end{aligned} \tag{53}$$

Intuitively, $d\langle X,Y\rangle(t)=c_X(t)c_Y(t)^{\mathrm{T}}dt^2$ is the instantaneous covariance between $X(t)$ and $Y(t)$. We can conveniently express it in the form

$$c_X(t)c_Y(t)^{\mathrm{T}}=\rho_{X,Y}(t)\sigma_X(t)\sigma_Y(t), \tag{54}$$

where $\sigma_X(t)=\sqrt{c_X(t)c_X(t)^{\mathrm{T}}}$ is the instantaneous volatility of $X(t)$, and where $\rho_{X,Y}(t)$ is the instantaneous correlation coefficient between $X(t)$ and $Y(t)$. Notice that

$$c(t)\Big(\frac{c_M(t)}{M(t)}-\frac{c_N(t)}{N(t)}\Big)dt=dX(t)\,d\log\frac{M(t)}{N(t)}, \tag{55}$$

and so the change of the drift formula under the change of numeraire formula can be stated in the elegant, easy-to-remember form:

$$\begin{aligned}\mu_X^{\mathsf{Q}}(t)-\mu_X^{\mathsf{P}}(t)&=\frac{d}{dt}\langle X,\log\frac{M}{N}\rangle(t)\\&=\rho_{X,\log M}(t)\sigma_X(t)\sigma_{\log M}(t)-\rho_{X,\log N}(t)\sigma_X(t)\sigma_{\log N}(t).\end{aligned} \tag{56}$$

The change in the drift of a state variable is thus equal to the difference between the covariation of this state variable with the logarithmic returns on the new numeraire and its covariation with the logarithmic returns on the old numeraire.

[2] Recall that $c_X(t)$ and $c_Y(t)$ are row vectors.

4 Riskless Bond Numeraires and Associated EMMs

In this section, we discuss a number of important examples of numeraires used in financial engineering. These numeraires are tradeable instruments sensitive to various *interest rates*. Interest rates reflect the cost of borrowing funds, and their levels depend on a number of factors, such as the market conditions, term of the underlying loan, credit worthiness of the borrower, and others. In this section, we focus on rates whose levels and volatility reflect the market conditions only and are credit risk free.

We assume that rates-sensitive instruments are modeled within the stochastic framework as described in Section 3 as a complete market model. The basic component of an interest rate model is the *instantaneous forward rate* process $f(t,s)$. Its value is the future instantaneous interest rate at a future time s (i.e. the rate for the infinitesimally short term $[s, s+ds]$, observed at time $t \leq s$).

A *zero coupon bond* settling at time T_0 and maturing at $T > T_0$ is the process

$$P(t, T_0, T) = \exp\big(-\int_{T_0}^{T} f(t,s)ds\big), \tag{57}$$

for $t \leq T_0$. In other words, it is the time T_0 value of \$1 delivered (without a risk of default) at T, as observed at time $t \leq T_0$. Its current value is given by

$$P_0(T_0, T) = \mathsf{E}[P(T_0, T)], \tag{58}$$

where the expectation is taken with respect to a suitable measure.

4.1 Bank Account Numeraire

The *bank account numeraire* (or *spot numeraire*) is simply the value of a \$1 deposited in a bank and accruing the (credit riskless) instantaneous rate. In reality, the bank credits interest to the account daily, but this can be very well approximated by a continuous process.[3] The associated stochastic price process $N_0(t)$ is given by

$$N_0(t) = \exp\big(\int_0^t r(s)ds\big). \tag{59}$$

Here, the *spot rate* $r(t)$ is the instantaneous forward rate observed at the time it settles, that is,

$$r(t) = f(t,t). \tag{60}$$

The corresponding EMM, denoted by Q_0, is called the *spot measure*.

[3] This approximation breaks down if the economy is in a hyperinflation.

The special case of a constant riskless rate $r(t) = r$ plays a key role in the Black–Scholes model, and the banking account numeraire is the riskless bond $B(t)$ mentioned before. Valuation under this measure is referred to as *risk neutral* valuation.

4.2 Forward Numeraire

The *T-forward numeraire* is simply the zero coupon bond for maturity T. Its price process is given by

$$\begin{aligned} N_T(t) &= P(t,t,T) \\ &= \exp\Big(-\int_t^T f(t,s)ds\Big), \end{aligned} \tag{61}$$

for $t < T$. This numeraire arises naturally in pricing instruments based on term forward rates maturing at time T.

Term (e.g. three months) forward rates for settlement at T_0 and maturity at T are defined by the equation

$$P(t,T_0,T) = \frac{1}{1+\delta F(t,T_0,T)}, \tag{62}$$

where δ is the contractually specified *day count fraction* for the accrual period from T_0 to T[4]. Importantly, $F(t,T_0,T)$ can be modeled as a martingale under the equivalent martingale measure associated with N_T. Indeed, it is easy to see that

$$F(t,T_0,T) = \frac{P(t,t,T_0) - P(t,t,T)}{P(t,t,T)}. \tag{63}$$

Consequently, $F(t,T_0,T)$ is the value of a portfolio of tradeable assets, and thus itself tradeable, expressed in the units of $N_T(t)$. According to Section 3.4, there exists a unique measure under which $F(t,T_0,T)$ is a martingale. This EMM is called the *T-forward measure* and denoted by Q_T.

4.3 Annuity Numeraire

Consider a forward starting *interest rate swap* (IRS) which settles in T_0 and matures in T years from now. An IRS is a transaction between two counterparties who exchange interest payments on an agreed notional principal.

On a vanilla swap, fixed coupon interest payments are exchanged for floating rate payments. For the sake of simplicity, we assume that the payment dates on the fixed and floating legs of the swap are the same, and that the floating rate is the same as the discounting rate. The former of these assumptions is a minor

[4] Approximately, $\delta = T - S$.

simplification, made to lighten up the notation only. The latter is an important simplification, as the *basis* between the floating rate and the discounting rate may exhibit a complex dynamics.

Let S be the fixed rate, let $T_1 < T_2 < \ldots < T_m = T$ denote the coupon payment dates of (the fixed leg of) the swap, and let T^v denote the valuation date. The cash flows on the fixed leg of a swap are given by

$$\begin{aligned}\mathrm{FIXED}(t, T^v, T_{0:m}) &= S\sum_{j=1}^{m}\delta_j P(t, T^v, T_j)\\ &= SA(t, T^v, T_{0:m}),\end{aligned}$$

where δ_j denotes the day count fraction associated with the accrual period from T_{j-1} to $T_j, j = 1, \ldots, n$, and where $T_{0:m}$ denotes the set of dates $T_0, T_1, \ldots, T_m$. The process $A(t, T^v, T_{0:m})$ is the *annuity function* (or the dvo1) of the swap defined by:

$$A(t, T^v, T_{0:m}) = \sum_{j=1}^{m}\delta_j P(t, T^v, T_j). \tag{64}$$

The cash flows on the floating leg are

$$\begin{aligned}\mathrm{FLOAT}(t, T^v, T_{0:m}) &= \sum_{j=1}^{m}\delta_j F(t, T_{j-1}, T_j)P(t, T^v, T_j)\\ &= P(t, T^v, T_0) - P(t, T^v, T).\end{aligned}$$

The *annuity numeraire* associated with this swap is defined as the price process of the annuity function observed on the valuation date,

$$N_{T_{0:m}}(t) = A(t, t, T_{0:m}). \tag{65}$$

The annuity is an asset that pays \$1 (per annum) on each coupon payment day of the swap, accrued according to the swap's day count day convention. The *break-even swap rate* is the fixed rate which renders the value of the swap zero:

$$S(t, T_{0:m}) = \frac{P(t, t, T_0) - P(t, t, T)}{A(t, t, T_{0:m})}. \tag{66}$$

Notice that the swap rate is a martingale if the annuity is used as a numeraire: it is the price of the portfolio consisting of two zero coupon bonds (long and short) expressed in the units of the annuity numeraire. The EMM $\mathsf{Q}_{T_{0:m}}$ associated with this numeraire is called the *(forward) swap measure*. The annuity numeraire arises as the natural numeraire when valuing swaptions. It is the mechanism that allows us to link the swaption as an option on a swap to the option on the corresponding swap rate.

For marking to market purposes we need to calculate the expected values of both legs of the swap. For simplicity, we will conduct the calculation under the spot measure. The expected value under Q_0 of the fixed leg is, given by

$$\begin{aligned} V_{\text{fixed}}(T^v) &= S\mathsf{E}^{Q_0}[A(0,T^v,T_{0:m})] \\ &= S\sum_{j=1}^{m}\delta_j P_0(T^v,T_j) \\ &= SA_0(T^v,T_{0:m}). \end{aligned} \tag{67}$$

Here, and in the following, we use the notation $P_0(T^v,T) = \mathsf{E}^{Q_0}[P(0,T^v,T)]$: that is $P_0(T^v,T)$ denotes the currently observed (nonstochastic) value of the zero coupon bond. Also, by

$$A_0(T^v,T_{0:m}) = \sum_{j=1}^{m}\delta_j P_0(T^v,T_j)$$

we denote the current (nonstochastic) value of the annuity function. The expected value of the floating leg is given by

$$V_{\text{float}}(T^v) = P_0(T^v,T_0) - P_0(T^v,T). \tag{68}$$

The expected value of the swap rate process

$$S_0(T_{0:m}) = \mathsf{E}^{Q_{T_{0:m}}}\left[S(T_0,T_{0:m})\right] \tag{69}$$

is the currently observed value of the swap rate for the settlement T_0, and is called the *forward swap rate*. Notice that its value does not depend on the valuation date T^v and we suppress it from our notation.

The forward swap rate can be expressed in terms of the current market data as follows. Using (40), we find that

$$\begin{aligned} \mathsf{E}^{Q_{T_{0:m}}}\left[S(T_0,T_{0:m})\right] &= \mathsf{E}^{Q_{T_{0:m}}}\left[\frac{\text{FLOAT}(T_0,T_0,T_{0:m})}{A(T_0,T_0,T_{0:m})}\right] \\ &= \frac{1}{N_{T_{0:m}}(0)}\left(N_{T_{0:m}}(0)\mathsf{E}^{Q_{T_{0:m}}}\left[\frac{\text{FLOAT}(T_0,T_0,T_{0:m})}{N_{T_{0:m}}(T_0)}\right]\right) \\ &= \frac{1}{N_{T_{0:m}}(0)}\left(N_0(0)\mathsf{E}^{Q_0}\left[\frac{\text{FLOAT}(T_0,T_0,T_{0:m})}{N_0(T_0)}\right]\right). \end{aligned}$$

Using the fact that $N_0(0) = 1$ and

$$\frac{\text{FLOAT}(T_0,T_0,T_{0:m})}{N_0(T_0)} = \text{FLOAT}(0,0,T_{0:m}),$$

we find that

$$\begin{aligned} S_0(T_{0:m}) &= \frac{\mathsf{E}^{\mathsf{Q}_0}[\mathrm{FLOAT}(0,0,T_{0:m})]}{\mathsf{E}^{\mathsf{Q}_0}[A(0,0,T_{0:m})]} \\ &= \frac{V_{\mathrm{float}}(0)}{A_0(0,T_{0:m})}. \end{aligned} \tag{70}$$

The forward swap rate (i.e. the expected value of the future swap rate under the swap measure) is given by the ratio of the current value of the floating leg and the current value of the annuity function.

5 Change of Numeraire in Interest Rate and FX Models

Choice of a numeraire is a matter of convenience and is dictated by the valuation problem at hand. Asset valuation frequently leads to complicated stochastic processes, and one way of making the problem easier is to eliminate the drift term from the stochastic differential equation defining the process. The change of numeraire technique allows us to achieve precisely this: modify the probability law (the measure) of the process so that, under this new measure, the process is driftless (i.e. it is a martingale). From the financial perspective, this results in *convexity adjustments* to various rates and spreads defined under non-martingale measures [22].

5.1 CMS and Change from Forward Measure to Swap Measure

The *constant maturity swap rate* (CMS rate) is a floating rate used in a number of interest rate derivative instruments. Unlike a short-term (say, three-month) rate, the CMS rate references a swap rate, and is thus used by entities which require to manage their exposure to longer dated rates.

The CMS rate is defined as the rate entering the following forward contract. The counterparties choose the contract settlement date T_0 and the reference swap settling on this date, say the 10-year swap, which matures on date T. On date T_0 the counterparties observe the fixing $S(T_{0:m})$ of the break-even rate on the reference swap. The payoff of the transaction is the difference between a strike rate K and the swap rate fixing, accruing over the fraction δ of the year, applied to the agreed upon notional, and payable on date $T^p \geq T_0$. The value of the strike rate that renders this transaction worth zero is called the CMS rate.

Mathematically, the CMS rate $\mathbf{S}$ referenced by the swap with coupon dates $T_{0:m}$ and payable on T^p is determined by the break-even condition:

$$P_0(0,T^p)K\delta - P_0(0,T^p)\mathsf{E}^{\mathsf{Q}_{T^p}}[S(T_{0:m})]\delta = 0. \tag{71}$$

Consequently, the fair value of the strike rate is given by

$$\mathrm{CMS}(T_{0:m}; T^p) = \mathsf{E}^{\mathsf{Q}_{T^p}}[S(T_{0:m})]. \tag{72}$$

Our goal is to express (72) in a terms of the expected value under the swap measure. Let $A(t, T_{0:m}) = A(t, t, T_{0:m})$ denote the forward annuity function process defined in (64), which serves as the natural numeraire for the swap rate process. Now, from the pricing law (40) and the expression for the Radon–Nikodym derivative in terms of the numeraires (42), we infer that

$$\begin{aligned} P_0(0, T^p)\mathsf{E}^{\mathsf{Q}_{T^p}}[S(T_{0:m})] &= P_0(0, T^p)\mathsf{E}^{\mathsf{Q}_{T^p}}\Big[\frac{S(T_{0:m})P(T_0, T^p)}{P(T_0, T^p)}\Big] \\ &= A_0(0, T_{0:m})\mathsf{E}^{\mathsf{Q}}\Big[\frac{S(T_{0:m})P(T_0, T^p)}{A(T_{0:m})}\Big]. \end{aligned}$$

Therefore, from (72) we infer that

$$\begin{aligned} \mathrm{CMS}(T_{0:m}; T^p) &= \mathsf{E}^{\mathsf{Q}_{T^p}}[S(T_{0:m})] \\ &= \mathsf{E}^{\mathsf{Q}_{T_{0:m}}}\Big[S(T_{0:m})\,\frac{A_0(0, T_{0:m})}{A(T_{0:m})}\,\frac{P(T_0, T^p)}{P_0(T_0, T^p)}\Big]. \end{aligned} \tag{73}$$

This somewhat complicated expression can be interpreted as follows. We write

$$\frac{A_0(0, T_{0:m})}{A(T_{0:m})}\,\frac{P(T_0, T^p)}{P_0(T_0, T^p)} = 1 + \Big(\frac{A_0(0, T_{0:m})}{A(T_{0:m})}\,\frac{P(T_0, T^p)}{P_0(T_0, T^p)} - 1\Big).$$

Notice that, by the martingale property of the swap measure,

$$\mathsf{E}^{\mathsf{Q}_{T_{0:m}}}[S(T_{0:m})] = S_0(T_{0:m}),$$

where $S_0(T_{0:m}) = S(0, T_{0:m})$ is the current value of the forward swap rate. As a result,

$$\begin{aligned} \mathrm{CMS}(T_{0:m}; T^p) &= S_0(T_{0:m}) + \mathsf{E}^{\mathsf{Q}_{T_{0:m}}}\Big[S(T_{0:m})\Big(\frac{A_0(0, T_{0:m})}{A(T_{0:m})}\,\frac{P(T_0, T^p)}{P_0(T_0, T^p)} - 1\Big)\Big] \\ &= S_0(T_{0:m}) + \Delta(T_{0:m}; T^p), \end{aligned}$$

where $\Delta(T_{0:m}; T^p)$ denotes the *CMS convexity adjustment*, that is the difference between the (current) forward swap rate and the CMS rate.

The expression for the CMS convexity adjustment derived in the previous two paragraphs is model independent, and one has to make choices in order to produce a workable value. The issue of accurate calculation of the CMS adjustments is of great practical importance and has been the subject of ongoing research.

Assume a complete n-factor market model for the swap rate, driven by an n-dimensional Brownian motion. Choosing the swap measure, the process for the swap rate S reads

$$dS(t) = c_S(t)dW^{Q_{T_{0:m}}}(t). \tag{74}$$

Under the forward measure Q_{T^P}, the process for S acquires a drift:

$$dS(t) = \mu_{CMS}(t)dt + c_S(t)dW^{Q_{T^P}}(t). \tag{75}$$

Equation (52) (or (56)) yields

$$\mu_{CMS}(t) = \rho_{S,\log P}(t)\sigma_S(t)\sigma_{\log P}(t) - \rho_{S,\log A}(t)\sigma_S(t)\sigma_{\log A}(t).$$

The drift has thus two components: one depending on the correlation between the swap rate and the annuity, and one depending on the correlation between the swap rate and the discount to payment day. Its exact form depends, of course, on the detailed specification of the model of the swap rate. Practical one- and two-factor models along these lines are discussed in [11], [14], and [9].

5.2 FMM Term Structure Model

Interest rates exhibit a complex structure reflecting their dependence on the terms of the underlying loans. Their mathematical modeling, involving a suitable concept of a "rates curve," is an attempt at capturing the multifactor dynamics of the rates and their interdependences. Depending on model specification, the curve can be built out of market observables, such as par swap rates (or, simply, swap rates), or calculated quantities such as the instantaneous rate.

The industry standard for interest rates modeling is the Forward Market Model (FMM), formerly known as LIBOR Market Model (LMM). Unlike the older approaches (short rate models), where the underlying state variable is the instantaneous spot rate, FMM captures the dynamics of the curve of interest rates by using as its state variables the market observable term (say, three-month) forwards of a benchmark rate. Extensive discussion of the FMM model, including methodologies for its calibration to market data and uses for pricing and risk management of interest rate derivatives, can be found in [5] and [23].

As the capital markets are currently in transition moving away from LIBOR to other benchmark rates, we chose to refer to this model as FMM, without specifying that benchmark rate, as long as it is a forward-looking term rate. In the US dollar market, SOFR is emerging as the LIBOR replacement. SOFR is an overnight rate and so a term rate is intrinsically backward-looking [19], but a market for forward-looking term forward rates has been rapidly developing.

The time evolution of the forwards is given by a set of stochastic differential equations in a way that guarantees arbitrage freeness of the process. The model is intrinsically multifactor, meaning that it has the capacity to capture accurately various aspects of the curve dynamics such as parallel shifts, steepenings/flattenings, and butterflies.

Specifically, we consider a sequence of approximately equally spaced dates $0 = T_0 < T_1 < \ldots < T_N$, which will be termed the *standard tenors*. A standard forward rate $F_j, j = 0, 1, \ldots, N-1$ is associated with a forward rate agreement which starts on T_j and matures on T_{j+1}. In the context of the US dollar market, it is usually assumed that $N = 120$ and the F_j's are three-month forward rates.

Each forward F_j is modeled as a continuous time stochastic process $F_j(t)$. This process gets killed at $t = T_j$, as the forward rate fixes. The dynamics of the forward process is driven by an N-dimensional, correlated Brownian motion $W_1(t), \ldots, W_{N-1}(t)$. We let ρ_{jk} denote the correlation coefficient between $W_j(t)$ and $W_k(t)$:

$$dW_j(t)dW_k(t) = \rho_{jk}dt\,.$$

We formulate the stochastic dynamics of the forwards as a system of stochastic differential equations:

$$dF_j(t) = \mu_j(F(t), t)dt + c_j(F_j(t), t)dW_j(t), \tag{76}$$

with suitably specified drift and diffusion coefficients $\mu_j(F(t), t)$ and $c_j(F_j(t), t)$, respectively. Commonly made choices of $c_j(F_j(t), t)$ are:

(i) $c_j(F_j(t), t) = \sigma_j(t)F_j(t)$ (lognormal model),
(ii) $c_j(F_j(t), t) = \sigma_j(t)$ (normal model), and
(iii) $c_j(F_j(t), t) = \sigma_j(t)F_j(t)^\beta$, $\beta < 1$ (CEV model),

where each $\sigma_j(t)$ is a deterministic function.

As discussed in Section 3, the *no arbitrage* requirement of asset pricing forces a relationship between the drift coefficient $\mu_j(F(t), t)$ and the diffusion coefficient: the form of the drift term depends thus on the choice of numeraire. In fact, this condition determines it completely!

Recall from Section 4.2 that F_k is a martingale under the T_{k+1}-forward measure Q_k, and so its dynamics reads:

$$dF_k(t) = c_k(F_k(t), t)dW_k(t).$$

Since the j-th forward settles at T_j, the process for $F_j(t)$ is killed at $t = T_j$. We shall determine the drifts $\mu_j(F(t), t)$ by requiring lack of arbitrage.

Let us first assume that $j < k$. The numeraires for the measures Q_j and Q_k are the prices $P\left(t, T_{j+1}\right)$ and $P\left(t, T_{k+1}\right)$ of the zero coupon bonds expiring at T_{j+1} and T_{k+1}, respectively. Explicitly,

$$P(t, T_{j+1}) = P(t, T_{g(t)}) \prod_{i=g(t)}^{j} \frac{1}{1 + \delta_i F_i(t)}, \tag{77}$$

where the index $g(t)$ is defined by $g(t) = m+1$ if $T_m \leq t < T_{m+1}$. Here $P(t, T_{g(t)})$ denotes the "stub" discount factor over the incomplete accrual period from t through $T_{g(t)}$. Since the drift of $F_j(t)$ under Q_j is zero, equation (52) yields:

$$
\begin{aligned}
\mu_j(F(t), t)dt &= d\left\langle F_j, \log \frac{P(T_{k+1})}{P(T_{j+1})}\right\rangle(t) \\
&= -dF_j(t)\, d\log \prod_{i=j+1}^{k} (1 + \delta_i F_i(t)) \\
&= -\sum_{i=j+1}^{k} dF_j(t) \frac{\delta_i dF_i(t)}{1 + \delta_i F_i(t)} \\
&= -c_j(F_j(t), t) \sum_{i=j+1}^{k} \frac{\rho_{ji}\delta_i c_i(F_i(t), t)}{1 + \delta_i F_i(t)},
\end{aligned}
$$

where, in the last line, we have used (76) and the fact that $dW_i(t)dt = dt^2 = 0$. Similarly, for $j > k$, we find that

$$
\mu_j(F(t), t) = c_j(F_j(t), t) \sum_{i=k+1}^{j} \frac{\rho_{ji}\delta_i c_i(F_i(t), t)}{1 + \delta_i F_i(t)}.
$$

We can thus summarize this discussion as follows. We let $dW_j(t) = dW_j^{Q_k}(t)$ denote the Brownian motion under the measure Q_k. Then the dynamics of the FMM model is given by the following system of stochastic differential equations. For $t < \min(T_k, T_j)$,

$$
dF_j(t) = c_j(F_j(t), t) \times \begin{cases} -\sum_{i=j+1}^{k} \frac{\rho_{ji}\delta_i c_i(F_i(t), t)}{1 + \delta_i F_i(t)}\, dt + dW_j(t), & \text{if } j < k, \\ dW_j(t), & \text{if } j = k, \\ \sum_{i=k+1}^{j} \frac{\rho_{ji}\delta_i c_i(F_i(t), t)}{1 + \delta_i F_i(t)}\, dt + dW_j(t), & \text{if } j > k. \end{cases} \tag{78}
$$

These equations are subject to the initial condition:

$$
F_j(0) = F_{j0}, \tag{79}
$$

where F_{j0} is the current value of the forward, for all j. The form of the drift coefficients in (78) has been uniquely determined by (i) the requirement that each $F_j(t)$ is a martingale under a suitable measure, and (ii) the relation linking the drift coefficients for the dynamics of $F_j(t)$ under two equivalent measures.

Practical application of this model requires a lot of work: this is not a surprise given its complexity. As it stands, the model involves a vast number of parameters and its dynamics is driven by a high dimensional Brownian motion. In order that the model is workable, reasonable approximations to its full structure have to be made; see [5], [23].

5.3 Foreign Exchange Markets and Quanto Adjustment

We now consider two financial markets: *domestic* and *foreign*, defined in terms of the corresponding probability spaces $(\Omega^d, \mathscr{F}^d, \mathsf{P}^d)$ and $(\Omega^f, \mathscr{F}^f, \mathsf{P}^f)$, both arbitrage free and complete in the sense of Section 3. Assets trading in these markets are denominated in the respective local currencies: domestic or foreign. Consider a contingent claim on an asset trading in the foreign market, whose value is denominated in the domestic currency. Modeling this transaction requires that we express the dynamics of the foreign transaction under the domestic measure. This leads to a drift adjustment in the dynamics of the foreign asset called the *quanto adjustment*. The quanto adjustment measures the impact of the correlation between the *foreign exchange (FX) rate* and the price of the asset on the value of a cross-currency transaction.

Let Q^d and Q^f denote the EMMs corresponding to suitably chosen numeraires N^d and N^f, respectively. Finally, let X denote the FX rate between the two markets defined as

$$X^{d/f} = \frac{\text{\# of units of domestic currency}}{\text{one unit of foreign currency}}. \tag{80}$$

Note that $X^{f/d} = 1/X^{d/f}$.

We consider a contingent claim $V = V^f$ expiring at T, denominated in the foreign currency. Then both $V^f(t)/N^f(t)$ and $X^{d/f}(t)V^f(t)/N^d(t)$ are martingales. Then

$$\begin{aligned} V^d(s) &= X^{d/f}(s)V^f(s) \\ &= X^{d/f}(s)N^f(s)\mathsf{E}^{\mathsf{Q}^f}\Big[\frac{V^f(T)}{N^f(T)}\,|\mathscr{F}_s^f\Big]. \end{aligned}$$

On the other hand,

$$\begin{aligned} V^d(s) &= N^d(s)\mathsf{E}^{\mathsf{Q}^d}\Big[\frac{V^d(T)}{N^d(T)}\,|\mathscr{F}_s^d\Big] \\ &= N^d(s)\mathsf{E}^{\mathsf{Q}^d}\Big[\frac{X^{d/f}(T)V^f(T)}{N^d(T)}\,|\mathscr{F}_s^d\Big] \\ &= N^d(s)\mathsf{E}^{\mathsf{Q}^f}\Big[\frac{X^{d/f}(T)V^f(T)}{N^d(T)}\,\frac{d\mathsf{Q}^d}{d\mathsf{Q}^f}(T)\,|\mathscr{F}_s^f\Big]. \end{aligned}$$

This yields the following expression for the Radon–Nikodym derivative of these two measures:

$$\begin{aligned}\frac{dQ^d}{dQ^f}(t) &= \frac{N^d(t)}{X^{d/f}(t)N^f(t)}\frac{X^{d/f}(0)N^f(0)}{N^d(0)}\\ &= \frac{X^{f/d}(t)N^d(t)}{N^f(t)}\frac{N^f(0)}{X^{f/d}(0)N^d(0)}.\end{aligned} \tag{81}$$

As special cases of this equation, we consider the following two examples.

EXAMPLE. Assume first that the numeraires are the running banking accounts in both currencies,

$$\begin{aligned}N_0^d(t) &= \exp\Big(\int_0^t r^d(s)ds\Big),\\ N_0^f(t) &= \exp\Big(\int_0^t r^f(s)ds\Big),\end{aligned} \tag{82}$$

where $r^d(t)$ and $r^f(t)$ denote the domestic and foreign short rates, respectively. Then

$$\begin{aligned}\frac{dQ_0^d}{dQ_0^f}(t) &= \frac{X^{d/f}(0)}{X^{d/f}(t)}\frac{N^{d_0}(t)}{N^{f_0(t)}}\\ &= \frac{X^{d/f}(0)}{X^{d/f}(t)}\exp\Big(\int_0^t (r^d(s)-r^f(s))ds\Big).\end{aligned} \tag{83}$$

EXAMPLE. Assume that the numeraires are the zero coupon bonds $N_T^d(t) = P^d(t,T)$ and $N_T^f(t) = P^f(t,T)$ in both currencies, with the corresponding EMMs Q_T^d and Q_T^f. Then

$$\frac{dQ_T^d}{dQ_T^f}(t) = \frac{X^{d/f}(0)}{X^{d/f}(t)}\frac{P^d(t,T)}{P^d(0,T)}\frac{P^f(0,T)}{P^f(t,T)}. \tag{84}$$

Assume now that the exchange rate $X = X^{d/f}$ follows the following process under the measure Q^f:

$$dX(t) = \mu_X(t)dt + c_X(t)dW^f(t), \tag{85}$$

and that the dynamics of the foreign asset $V(t)$ is given by

$$dV(t) = \mu_V^f(t)dt + c_V(t)dW^f(t). \tag{86}$$

Then the quanto adjusted dynamics for the foreign asset denominated in the domestic currency $V^d(t)$ is given by

$$dV^d(t) = \big(\mu_V^f(t) + \rho_{X,V}(t)\sigma_{\log X}(t)\sigma_{\log V}(t)\big)dt + c_V(t)dW^f(t), \tag{87}$$

where $\rho_{X,V}(t)$ denotes the instantaneous correlation coefficients between the FX rate and the asset. The drift coefficient in the dynamics of the asset is adjusted by a term proportional to the correlation coefficient $\rho_{X,V}(t)$.

6 Incomplete Markets

The market modeling framework as defined in Section 3.1 may be inadequate in specific applications. A variety of reasons may be responsible for this, and a large volume of research has been devoted to refining this framework. A good deal of criticism of the model focuses on the assumption that Brownian motion is assumed to be the driver of risk, and models have been developed that relax this assumption. Alternatively, models have been proposed and adopted by the industry, in which the primary risk drivers remain Brownian motions, but additional, unobservable state variables are introduced whose purpose is to explain market phenomena not captured by the framework of Section 3.1. By their very nature, these models are *incomplete*, as each of the state variables is driven by its own source of stochasticity.

Incomplete models are discussed in detail in [27] and [2], but we are not striving here for that level of generality. Instead, in this section we will focus on three specific instances of such incomplete market models, namely stochastic volatility, credit risk, and prepayment risk.

6.1 Stochastic Volatility

Stochastic volatility models attempt to remedy one of the key deficiencies of the Black–Scholes model, namely its inability to capture the dependence of the implied option volatility on the strike. This dependence is referred to as the *option smile*, and its presence has important implications for pricing and risk management.

As an example, we consider the SABR model of stochastic volatility [12]. We consider a tradeable asset $F(t)$ (usually assumed to be a forward asset, such as a forward rate or price), which is driven by a Brownian motion $W(t)$. The instantaneous volatility parameter in the dynamics of that asset is assumed to be given by a diffusion process $\sigma(t)$ driven by another Brownian motion, $Z(t)$. It is correlated with $W(t)$ according to

$$dW(t)dZ(t) = \rho dt, \tag{88}$$

where ρ is the correlation coefficient. The dynamics of the SABR model is given by the system:

$$\begin{aligned} dF(t) &= \sigma(t)c(F(t))dW(t), \\ d\sigma(t) &= \alpha\sigma(t)dZ(t). \end{aligned} \tag{89}$$

Here $c(x)$ is a function, called the *backbone* function, whose specification depends on the market for which the model is used. In the classic SABR model, the backbone function is $c(x) = x^\beta$, where $\beta \leq 1$. The SABR process is a martingale[5] under the measure associated with the two-dimensional Brownian motion $W(t), Z(t)$.

Notice that there are infinitely many probability measures under which the process $F(t)$ is a martingale. Indeed, we could assume that the process for $\sigma(t)$ has a prescribed drift:

$$d\sigma(t) = \delta(F(t), \sigma(t))dt + \alpha\sigma(t)dZ(t). \tag{90}$$

This drift coefficient could reflect, for instance, that implied volatility tends to be mean reverting. The presence of the drift term leads to option prices and their risk characteristics different from those derived from the original SABR model. As a consequence of Girsanov's theorem, the probability measure for the model with the drift is related to the original probability measure by the Radon–Nikodym derivative constructed as follows:

$$L(t) = \exp\Big(\int_0^t \theta(s)\, dW^\perp(s) - \frac{1}{2}\int_0^t \theta(s)^2\, ds\Big), \tag{91}$$

where

$$\theta(t) = \frac{\delta(F(t), \sigma(t))}{\alpha\sqrt{1-\rho^2}\,\sigma(t)}, \tag{92}$$

and where $W^\perp(t)$ is the component of $Z(t)$, which is independent of $W(t)$.

6.2 SABR-FMM Term Structure Model

The classic FMM model of Section 5.2 has a severe limitation: while it is possible to calibrate it to the market data, so that it closely matches at the money option prices, it generally misprices out of the money options. The main reason for this is its specification. While the market uses stochastic volatility models in order to price out of the money vanilla options (swaptions and caps/floors), FMM assumes nonstochastic volatility and so it is incompatible with vanilla option market prices. In order to remedy the problem, several versions of extended FMM have been proposed, which include the SABR dynamics as part of their specifications. Here we will discuss the version developed in [13] and [24].

In analogy with the single forward model discussed in Section 6.1, we assume that the instantaneous volatilities $c_j(F_j(t), \sigma_j(t), t)$ of the forward rates

[5] Strictly speaking, it is a *local martingale*. Stronger assumptions on the backbone function have to be made in order to assert that the process is a strict martingale.

F_j are functions of both $F_j(t)$ and the stochastic volatility parameter $\sigma_j(t)$. The choice analogous to the classic SABR model is

$$c_j(F_j(t), \sigma_j(t), t) = \sigma_j(t) L_j(t)^{\beta_j}. \tag{93}$$

Furthermore, we assume that, under the T_{k+1}-forward measure Q_k, the full dynamics of the forward is given by the stochastic system:

$$\begin{aligned} dF_k(t) &= c_k(F_k(t), \sigma_k(t), t) dW_k(t), \\ d\sigma_k(t) &= d_k(F_k(t), \sigma_k(t), t) dZ_k(t). \end{aligned} \tag{94}$$

The choice of

$$c_k(F_k(t), \sigma_k(t), t) = \alpha_k(t)\sigma_k(t). \tag{95}$$

where $\alpha_k(t)$ is a deterministic function of t is analogous to the classic SABR model. In addition, we impose the following instantaneous volatility structure:

$$dW_j(t) dZ_k(t) = r_{jk}\, dt, \tag{96}$$

and

$$dZ_j(t) dZ_k(t) = \eta_{jk} dt. \tag{97}$$

The block correlation matrix

$$\Pi = \begin{bmatrix} \rho & r \\ r^{\mathrm{T}} & \eta \end{bmatrix} \tag{98}$$

is assumed to be positive definite.

Let us now derive the dynamics of such an extended FMM model under the common forward measure Q_k. According to the arbitrage pricing theory, the form of the stochastic differential equations defining the dynamics of the forward rates depends on the choice of numeraire. Under the T_{k+1}-forward measure Q_k, the dynamics of the forward rate $L_j(t), j \neq k$ reads:

$$dF_j(t) = \mu_j(F(t), \sigma_j(t), t) dt + c_j(F_j(t), \sigma_j(t), t) dW_j(t).$$

We determine the drifts $\mu_j(F(t), \sigma_j(t), t)$ by requiring absence of arbitrage. The argument is essentially identical to the derivation of the drift terms for the classic FMM, and we can thus summarize the result as follows. Denoting by $W_k(t) = W^{Q_k}(t)$ the Brownian motion under the measure Q_k, we find that

$$dF_j(t) = c_j(F_j(t), \sigma_j(t), t) \times \begin{cases} -\sum_{i=j+1}^{k} \dfrac{\rho_{ji}\delta_i c_i(F_i(t), \sigma_i(t), t)}{1 + \delta_i F_i(t)} dt + dW_j(t), & \text{if } j < k, \\ dW_j(t), & \text{if } j = k, \\ \sum_{i=k+1}^{j} \dfrac{\rho_{ji}\delta_i c_i(F_i(t), \sigma_i(t), t)}{1 + \delta_i F_i(t)} dt + dW_j(t), & \text{if } j > k. \end{cases} \tag{99}$$

Let us now compute the drift coefficient $\nu_j(F(t), \sigma_j(t), t)$ for the dynamics of $\sigma_j(t), j \neq k$, under Q_k,

$$d\sigma_j(t) = \nu_j(F(t), \sigma_j(t), t)dt + d_j(F(t), \sigma_j(t), t)dZ_j(t).$$

Assume that $j < k$. The numeraires for the measures Q_j and Q_k are the prices $P\left(t, T_{j+1}\right)$ and $P(t, T_{k+1})$ of the zero coupon bonds maturing at T_{j+1} and T_{k+1}, respectively. Since the drift of $F_j(t)$ under Q_j is zero, equation (52):

$$\begin{aligned}
\nu_j(F(t), \sigma(t), t)dt &= d\left\langle \sigma_j, \log \frac{P(T_{j+1})}{P(T_{k+1})} \right\rangle(t) \\
&= -d\sigma_j(t)\, d\log \prod_{i=j+1}^{k} (1 + \delta_i F_i(t)) \\
&= -\sum_{i=j+1}^{k} d\sigma_j(t) \frac{\delta_i dF_i(t)}{1 + \delta_i F_i(t)} \\
&= -d_j(F_j(t), \sigma_j(t), t) \sum_{i=j+1}^{k} \frac{r_{ji}\delta_i c_i(F_i(t), \sigma_i(t), t)}{1 + \delta_i F_i(t)}\, dt.
\end{aligned}$$

Similarly, for $j > k$, we find that

$$\Gamma_j(t) = d_j(F_j(t), \sigma_j(t), t) \sum_{i=k+1}^{j} \frac{r_{ji}\delta_i c_i(F_i(t), \sigma_i(t), t)}{1 + \delta_i F_i(t)}.$$

This leads to the following system of stochastic differential equations under the forward measure Q_k:

$$\begin{aligned}
d\sigma_j(t) &= d_j(F_j(t), \sigma_j(t), t) \\
&\times \begin{cases}
-\sum_{i=j+1}^{k} \frac{r_{ji}\delta_i c_i(F_i(t), \sigma_i(t), t)}{1 + \delta_i F_i(t)}\, dt + dZ_j(t), & \text{if } j < k, \\
dZ_j(t), & \text{if } j = k, \\
\sum_{i=k+1}^{j} \frac{r_{ji}\delta_i c_i(F_i(t), \sigma_i(t), t)}{1 + \delta_i F_i(t)}\, dt + dZ_j(t), & \text{if } j > k.
\end{cases}
\end{aligned} \tag{100}$$

These equations are subject to the initial conditions:

$$\begin{aligned}
F_j(0) &= F_{j0}, \\
\sigma_j(0) &= \sigma_{j0},
\end{aligned} \tag{101}$$

where F_{j0}'s and σ_{j0}'s are the currently observed values.

6.3 Event Risk and Event Intensity

A vast majority of fixed income instruments are subject to an *event risk*, in addition to interest rate risk. Over time, such events result in finitely many outcomes only, unlike stock prices or interest rates whose evolution may lead to a continuum of outcomes.

Two categories of event risk dominating the fixed income markets are[6]:

- *Credit risk*: a borrower's or a counterparty's failure to meet the delivery or payment obligations in accordance with agreed terms. This failure is referred to as a *default.*
- *Prepayment risk*: a borrower's decision to repay the loan early (in full or in part).

Both credit risk and prepayment risk are present in various types of mortgage-backed securities and asset-backed securities.

The basic probabilistic setup to model event risk is based on the concept of a random time τ, the *time to event*. The time to event represents the time instances at which an event occurs (such as an entity undergoing a default, or a borrower prepaying his loan). The stochastic indicator process $1_{\tau \leq t}$ defines a filtrated information set of the underlying probability space, which we denote by $(\mathcal{G}_t)_{t\geq 0}$.

The key concept to financial event modeling is that of a *counting processes*. A stochastic process $J(t)$ is called a counting process if:

(i) $J(t)$ is integer valued, nonnegative, with $J(0) = 0$.
(ii) Sample paths of $J(t)$ are right continuous, piecewise constant, may have jumps of size 1.

Jump times $\tau_1 < \tau_2 < \ldots$ are stopping times at which the process $J(t)$ increases by 1. The range of values of $J(t)$ may consist of two points $\{0, 1\}$, in case of simple defaults ("solvent," "in default") or prepayments ("not prepaid," "prepaid"). In case of modeling multistage default processes, such as in mortgage-backed securities, $J(t)$ may contain several values.

The *intensity* (also referred to as *hazard rate*) $\lambda(t)$ of $J(t)$ is defined by

$$\lambda(t)dt = \mathsf{P}(J(t + dt) - J(t) = 1 \mid \mathcal{G}_{t-}),$$

or alternatively,

$$\lambda(t)dt = \mathsf{E}[J(t + dt) - J(t) \mid \mathcal{G}_{t-}].$$

In other words, $\lambda(t)dt$ represents the conditional probability that an event occurs in the time interval $[t, t + dt]$ given the information up to time t. A counting process $J(t)$, whose intensity process $\lambda(t)$ is itself a diffusion process, is called a *Cox process*.

[6] For other categories of event risk in finance, see e.g. [7].

A Cox process $J(t)$ is associated with an information set generated by both $(\mathcal{G}_t)_{t>0}$ and $(\mathcal{F}_t)_{t>0}$, where $\mathcal{G}_t$ pertains to the "extrinsic" jump times dynamics, and where $\mathcal{F}_t$ refers to the "intrinsic" dynamics of the market. The event process and the intrinsic market process are not necessarily independent. The presence of the event risk thus causes the market model based on $S(t)$ and $J(t)$ to be incomplete.

In order to accommodate for the presence of even risk, we amend the framework of Section 3 in the following way [3].

(i) The probability of event depends only on the "intrinsic" information up to time t,

$$\mathsf{P}(\tau > t \,|\, \mathcal{F}_\infty) = \mathsf{P}(\tau > t \,|\, \mathcal{F}_t). \tag{102}$$

This assumption simply states that events are influenced only by the past history of the asset price.

(ii) There exists a doubly stochastic Cox process $\lambda(t)$ such that

$$\mathsf{P}(\tau > t \,|\, \mathcal{F}_t) = \exp\big(-\int_0^t \lambda(s)ds\big). \tag{103}$$

(iii) An event will eventually occur with probability 1,

$$\mathsf{P}(\tau < \infty) = 1. \tag{104}$$

Depending on the context, the intensity process $\lambda(t)$ represents the conditional default or prepayment probability density. The quantity

$$S(0,t) = \exp\left(-\int_0^t \lambda(s)ds\right) \tag{105}$$

is referred to as the *survival probability* (up to time t), and $Q(0,t) = 1 - S(0,t)$ is the *event probability*. Note that the survival probability itself is random, and hence models based on a stochastic hazard rate are often referred to as *doubly stochastic models*.

6.4 Credit Risk and Defaultable Numeraire

A prime example of financial event risk is *credit risk*, which is present in virtually all financial transactions. Credit risk is the potential that a borrower or a counterparty on a transaction will fail to meet its obligations according to agreed terms. This failure to deliver is referred to as a *default* event. The exact definition of what constitutes an event of default (bankruptcy, failure to pay coupon, failure to repay the principal, debt restructuring, etc.) is governed by strict legal language, and will not concern us here.

A basic synthetic credit sensitive instrument is a *credit default swap* (CDS). A CDS on a reference asset ("name") is a tradeable bilateral transaction in which one counterparty, the protection buyer, pays a periodic premium, while the other, the protection seller, pays the amount of *loss given default*, should the reference asset experience default during the term of the transaction.

A CDS is modeled within the framework of Section 6.3, with τ and $\lambda(t)$ denoting the time to default and default intensity, respectively. The discounted cash flows on the premium leg of a CDS are given by

$$\mathrm{PREM}(t, T^{\mathrm{v}}, T_{0:m}) = S\mathcal{A}(t, T^{\mathrm{v}}, T_{0:m}), \tag{106}$$

where S is the periodic premium rate, referred to as *credit spread*, and where $\mathcal{A}$ is the defaultable annuity function

$$\begin{aligned}\mathcal{A}(t, T^{\mathrm{v}}, T_{0:m}) = \sum_{j=1}^{n} \big(&\delta_j 1_{\tau > T_j}(t) P(t, T^{\mathrm{v}}, T_j) \\ &+ \tilde{\delta} 1_{T_j < \tau < T_{j+1}}(t) P(t, T^{\mathrm{v}}, \tau)\big).\end{aligned} \tag{107}$$

Here, T_0 is the settlement date, $T^{\mathrm{v}} \leq T_0$ is the valuation date, the summation runs over the premium payment dates of the swap, δ_j denotes the day count fraction associated with the period from T_{j-1} through T_j, and $\tilde{\delta}$ is the accrued premium between the date of default and the last premium payment date prior to the default.

The cash flow on the protection leg is triggered by a default event of the reference name, and it compensates the protection buyer for the loss on the par value of the underlying asset. Explicitly, it is given by

$$\mathrm{PROT}(t) = (1 - R(\tau)) 1_{\tau \leq T}(t) P(t, \tau), \tag{108}$$

where R denotes the *recovery rate*, defined as the par value of the reference name less the loss given default.

The process $N(t, T_{0:m}) = \mathcal{A}(t, t, T_{0:m})$ is referred to as the *defaultable annuity numeraire*. Note that, strictly speaking, $N(t, T_{0:m})$ is not a numeraire, as its value may be zero, if default occurs prior to T_0. The technical aspects related to this phenomenon were analyzed in [17] and [26], where it was shown that an equivalent martingale measure, called the *survival measure* and denoted by $\mathsf{Q}^{surv}_{T_{0:m}}$, can be defined.

The *par spread* S on a T-year CDS is the value of S for which the values of the premium leg and the protection leg are equal,

$$S(t, T_{0:m}) = \frac{\mathrm{PROT}(t)}{\mathcal{A}(t, t, T_{0:m})}. \tag{109}$$

$S(t, T_{0:m})$ is a martingale under the survival measure.

The expected value of the premium leg of a CDS is equal to[7]

$$\begin{aligned} V_{\text{prem}}(T^v) &= \mathcal{S}\mathsf{E}^{Q_0}\left[\mathcal{A}(T^v, T_{0:m})\right] \\ &= \mathcal{S}\sum_{j=1}^{n}\left(\delta_j \mathcal{P}_0(T^v, T_j) + \tilde{\delta}\mathcal{P}_0(T^v, \tau)\right) \\ &= \mathcal{S}\mathcal{A}_0(T^v, T_{0:m}), \end{aligned} \tag{110}$$

whereas the expected value of the protection leg is given by

$$\begin{aligned} V_{\text{prot}}(T^v) &= \mathsf{E}^{Q_0}\left[(1 - R(\tau))1_{\tau \le T}(t)P(T^v, \tau)\right] \\ &= \int_0^T \mathsf{E}^{Q_0}\left[(1 - R(s))\lambda(s)e^{-\int_{T^v}^{s}(r(t)+\lambda(t))dt}\right]ds. \end{aligned} \tag{111}$$

Here, $\mathcal{P}_0(T_1, T)$ denotes the value of a defaultable zero recovery zero coupon bond for maturity T given by

$$\begin{aligned} \mathcal{P}_0(T_1, T) &= \mathsf{E}^{Q_0}\left[1_{\tau > T}P(T_1, T)\right] \\ &= \mathsf{E}^{Q_0}\left[e^{-\int_{T_1}^{T}(r(t)+\lambda(t))dt}\right]. \end{aligned} \tag{112}$$

In particular, if rates and credit are independent, then

$$\mathcal{P}(T_1, T) = P(T_1, T)S(T_1, T), \tag{113}$$

where $S(T_1, T)$ denotes survival probability.

Today's value $\mathcal{S}_0(T_{0:m})$ of the forward par spread is given by the expected value of (109) under the survival measure. Reasoning as in Section 4.3, we find that

$$\mathcal{S}_0(T_{0:m}) = \frac{V_{prot}(0)}{\mathcal{A}_0(0, T_{0:m})}. \tag{114}$$

We can derive an approximate relation between the credit spread and the magnitude of credit intensity. To this end we first make the approximation:

$$\begin{aligned} \mathcal{A}(0, T_{0:m}) &\approx \int_0^T \mathsf{E}^{Q_0}\left[e^{-\int_0^t (r(s)+\lambda(s))ds}\right]dt \\ &= \int_0^T \mathcal{P}_0(0, t)dt. \end{aligned}$$

[7] Notice again that we are choosing to work with the spot measure for convenience; similar conclusions can be reached with a forward measure.

Assuming that the recovery rate is constant, we can approximate the value of the protection leg as follows:

$$\begin{aligned}&\int_0^T \mathsf{E}^{\mathsf{Q}_0}\left[(1-R(t))\lambda(t)e^{-\int_0^t (r(t)+\lambda(s))ds}\right]dt\\&\approx (1-R)\int_0^T \mathsf{E}^{\mathsf{Q}_0}\left[\lambda(t)e^{-\int_0^t (r(s)+\lambda(s))ds}\right]dt\\&=(1-R)\mathsf{E}^{\mathsf{Q}_0}\left[\lambda(T)\int_0^T e^{-\int_0^t (r(s)+\lambda(s))ds}dt-\int_0^T d\lambda(t)e^{-\int_0^t (r(s)+\lambda(s))ds}\right]\\&=(1-R)\mathsf{E}^{\mathsf{Q}_0}\left[\lambda(T)\int_0^T e^{-\int_0^t (r(s)+\lambda(s))ds}dt-\int_0^T \mu(t)e^{-\int_0^t (r(s)+\lambda(s))ds}dt\right],\end{aligned}$$

where in the third line we have integrated by parts. Assuming that the default intensity is close to constant with mean value $\bar{\lambda}$, and the drift is close to constant with mean value $\bar{\mu}$, we can further approximate as follows:

$$\begin{aligned}&\int_0^T \mathsf{E}^{\mathsf{Q}_0}\left[(1-R(t))\lambda(t)e^{-\int_0^t (r(t)+\lambda(s))ds}\right]dt\\&\qquad\approx (1-R)(\bar{\lambda}-\bar{\mu})\int_0^T \mathcal{P}_0(0,t)dt.\end{aligned}$$

As a consequence, we obtain the following *triangle relation*:

$$\mathcal{S}_0(T_{0:m})\approx(1-R)(\bar{\lambda}-\bar{\mu}), \tag{115}$$

which links the par spread to the hazard rate and recovery rate.

A *constant maturity credit default swap* (CMDS) is a variation on the CDS in which one leg pays a periodic floating (rather than fixed) coupon. This coupon is linked to the fixing of a reference spread on the previous coupon date. In order to elucidate the how this spread is calculated, consider a single period CMDS swap settling on T_0 and payment date T^p. For simplicity, we assume that there is no payment at time T^p if $T_0 \leq \tau < T^p$ (no accrued interest). The value of this coupon payment on the settlement date is

$$\mathcal{S}(T_0,T_{0:m})1_{\tau>T_0}P(T_0,T^p)$$

(multiplied by the day count fraction and the notional), and hence

$$\mathrm{CMDS}(T_{0:m};T^p)=\mathsf{E}^{\mathsf{Q}_{T^p}}\left[1_{\tau>T_0}\mathcal{S}(T_{0:m})\right]. \tag{116}$$

Using (40) and (42) we find that

$$\begin{aligned}\mathrm{CMDS}(T_{0:m};T^p)&=\mathsf{E}^{\mathsf{Q}_{T^p}}\left[1_{\tau>T_0}\mathcal{S}(T_{0:m})\right]\\&=\mathsf{E}^{\mathsf{Q}^{surv}_{T_{0:m}}}\left[\mathcal{S}(T_{0:m})\frac{\mathcal{A}_0(0,T_{0:m})}{\mathcal{A}(T_{0:m})}\frac{P(T_0,T^p)}{P_0(T_0,T^p)}\right],\end{aligned} \tag{117}$$

where $\mathsf{Q}^{surv}_{T_{0:m}}$ is the survival measure. Notice that $P(T_0,T^p)\neq 0$ and so the Radon–Nikodym derivative above is well defined.

In analogy with CMS, the CMDS spread can be expressed as the forward par spread plus a convexity adjustment. A practical method for evaluating the CMDS adjustment is presented in [1].

6.5 Cross Currency CDS and Quanto Spreads

A *quanto credit default swap* is a CDS in which default protection is purchased on a notional amount denominated in one currency (foreign), but the premium leg is denominated in a different currency (domestic). The difference between the par spreads on the quanto CDS and the corresponding CDS in the domestic currency is known as the *quanto CDS spread.* The quanto CDS spread reflects the dependence between the default intensity and the exchange rate between the two currencies. The effect is particularly pronounced in the case of sovereign CDSs, where it relates the risk between the "Twin Ds," default and (currency) devaluation.

The premium leg on a cross currency CDS is denominated in the domestic currency and is given by

$$\mathcal{S}^d \mathcal{A}^d(t, T^v, T_{0:m}),$$

where $\mathcal{S}^d$ is the par spread defined by (109). The protection leg is denominated in the foreign currency and is given by

$$(1 - R(\tau))1_{\tau \leq T}(t) P^f(t, \tau), \tag{118}$$

where R denotes the recovery rate.

Our objective is to determine the break-even par spread $\mathcal{S}^f$ denominated in the foreign currency. For simplicity, we assume that sudden currency devaluation is not possible, and so the process for X does not have a jump component. As in Section 5.3, assume that the FX rate $X = X^{d/f}(t)$ follow the process (85). Assume also that the reference name on the CDS has the default intensity process $\lambda^f(t)$ given by

$$d\lambda(t) = \mu^f_\lambda(t)dt + c_\lambda(t)dW^f(t), \tag{119}$$

under the foreign measure. The quanto credit spread is given by

$$\mathcal{S}^d_0(T_{0:m}) = \frac{V^d_{prot}(0)}{\mathcal{A}^d_0(0, T_{0:m})}. \tag{120}$$

Then, according to the calculations of Section 5.3, the drift of the intensity process in the domestic measure acquires a quanto adjustment measuring the impact of the correlation between the FX rate and the default intensity:

$$d\lambda^d(t) = \left(\mu^f_\lambda(t) + \rho_{\lambda,X}(t)\sigma_{\log\lambda}(t)\sigma_{\log X}(t)\right)dt + c_\lambda(t)dW^f(t). \tag{121}$$

This allows us to estimate the impact of the quanto effect on the spreads. Indeed, using the triangle equation (115), we obtain an approximate expression for the spread in the domestic currency:

$$S_0^d \approx S_0^f - (1 - R)\rho_{\lambda,X}\sigma_{\log\lambda}\sigma_{\log X}. \tag{122}$$

In other words, if the credit worthiness of the reference name is positively correlated with the domestic currency (meaning that the correlation coefficient $\rho_{\lambda,X}$ is negative), this causes the quanto credit spread to widen.

Specific models and practical methods for calculating the quanto CDS adjustments, including the possibility of currency devaluation, are presented in [4], [18], and [28].

6.6 Mortgage-Backed Securities and Prepayable Numeraire

Mortgage-backed securities (MBSs) are debt instruments whose cash flows are generated by pools of underlying collateral mortgage loans. In addition to interest rate risk, they carry a variety of event risks embedded in the collateral. Key of these risks is that a mortgage holder has the right to *prepay* the loan early. A borrower's decision to prepay is driven by factors which are only partly explained by the dynamics of interest rate. Any MBS model based solely on the interest process is thus incomplete, as it requires exogenous factors to capture the prepayment risk.

The basic instruments in the MBS market are *agency passthroughs*,[8] which are collateralized by conforming[9] thirty-year mortgage loans. A holder of a passthrough receives *all* the cash flows generated by the collateral, less the servicing and credit fees. These cash flows are uncertain because they are subject to prepayment risk. There is also a liquid market for futures contracts on passthroughs, called TBAs ("to be announced"), where each TBA is collateralized by (yet) unspecified pools of collateral. The scheduled cash flow on a TBA is $c_j = p_j + i_j^{\text{net}}$, where p_j is the scheduled principal repayment, and i_j^{net} is the interest less the servicing and credit spread F,

$$i_j^{\text{net}} = \frac{C}{12}\, b_{j-1},$$

where C is the *net coupon*, namely the rate on the mortgage loan with the servicing and credit fees deducted, and where b_j is the loan balance at the end of period j.

[8] The term "agency" refers here to one of the US Government Sponsored Entities, Freddie Mac or Fannie Mae.

[9] That is, satisfying certain credit and size requirements.

Consider a TBA collateralized by a pool of N mortgage loans. Typically, N is large, as a pool may consist of thousands of loans. By $\lambda_i(t)$ we denote the prepayment intensity of borrower $i = 1, \ldots, N$, we let τ_i denote the corresponding time to event, and we let $S_i(t, T)$ denote the individual survival probabilities. While the individual prepayment intensities are hard to observe, the effects of the weighted pool average

$$\lambda(t) = \sum_{i=1}^{N} w_j \lambda_i(t), \tag{123}$$

where the weights w_i reflect the original loan sizes, can be observed and quantified. We refer to $\lambda(t)$ as the prepayment intensity process of the TBA. Also,

$$S(t, T) = \sum_{i=1}^{N} w_i S_i(t, T) \tag{124}$$

is the initial balance weighted survival probability of the survival probabilities $S_i(t, T)$ in the pool.

Let T_0 be the settlement date of the TBA (called the *PSA date*), and let $T_1, \ldots, T_m$ denote the (monthly) coupon dates of the TBA. Somewhat schematically, the time t discounted cash flow on a TBA is thus given by[10]

$$\begin{aligned}
\text{TBA}(t) &= \sum_{j=1}^{m} P(t, T_0, T_j) \sum_{i=1}^{N} w_i \big(1_{\tau_i > T_{j-1}}(t) c_j + 1_{T_{j-1} < \tau_i < T_j}(t) b_j \big) \\
&= \sum_{j=1}^{m} P(t, T_0, T_j) \Big(\sum_{i=1}^{N} w_i 1_{\tau_i > T_{j-1}}(t)\, c_j + \sum_{i=1}^{N} w_i 1_{T_{j-1} < \tau_i < T_j}(t)\, b_j \Big),
\end{aligned}$$

where the scheduled payment by borrower i on the date T_j is denoted by c_{ij}, and b_{ij} denotes the outstanding loan balance of borrower i on that date. The term $1_{T_{j-1} < \tau_i < T_j}(t) b_{ij}$ represents the amount of cash prepaid over the period from T_{j-1} through T_j by borrower i.

The time t value of the TBA is given by the expected value of the cash flows:

$$\begin{aligned}
V(t) &= \mathsf{E}_t\big[\text{TBA}(t)\big] \\
&= \sum_{j=1}^{m} P(t, T_0, T_j) \big(S(t, T_{j-1})\, c_j + (S(t, T_{j-1}) - S(t, T_j)) b_j \big).
\end{aligned} \tag{125}$$

Alternatively, we can write this as

$$V(t) = \sum_{j=1}^{m} \mathfrak{P}(t, T_j)(c_j + \bar{\lambda}(T_{j-1}, T_j) b_j).$$

[10] For simplicity, we assume here that the TBA is brand new. For seasoned pools, it is necessary to take into account the *factor*, which accounts for the already repaid fraction of the principal.

Here, $\mathfrak{P}(t, T_0, T_j) = P(t, T_j)S(t, T_0, T_{j-1})$ is the *prepayable zero coupon bond* under the spot measure, and

$$\bar{\lambda}(T_{j-1}, T_j) = \frac{S(t, T_{j-1}) - S(t, T_j)}{S(t, T_{j-1})} \simeq \int_{T_{j-1}}^{T_j} \lambda(s) ds$$

is the conditional probability of prepayment in month j, also known as the *single month mortality* (SMM).

We divide up the cash flows of a TBA paying the (net) coupon C into *interest only* (IO) and *principal only* (PO) parts:

$$\mathrm{IO}(t) = \frac{C}{12}\mathfrak{A}(t, T_{0:m}), \tag{126}$$

and

$$\mathrm{PO}(t) = \sum_{j=1}^{m} P(t, T_0, T_j) \sum_{i=1}^{N} w_i (p_j + 1_{T_{j-1} < \tau_i < T_j}(t)\, b_j), \tag{127}$$

respectively. Here

$$\mathfrak{A}(t, T_{0:m}) = \sum_{j=1}^{m} P(t, T_0, T_j) \sum_{i=1}^{N} w_i 1_{\tau_i > T_{j-1}}(t)\, b_j \tag{128}$$

is the *amortizing annuity function*. Notice that the cash flows on the PO consist of both scheduled principal repayments and prepaid balances.

The *mortgage measure* is defined as the martingale measure corresponding to the amortizing numeraire $\mathfrak{N}_{T_{0:m}}(t) = \mathfrak{A}(t, T_{0:m})$. As in the case of the defaultable numeraire, the amortizing numeraire is not guaranteed to be positive for all t before the settlement: it is conceivable (if extremely unlikely) that all loans prepay. Currently, no market for prepayment swaps or swaptions exists. Should such a market ever come to existence, the amortizing annuity and mortgage measure would play the same practical role as the annuities and the corresponding EMMs in the interest rate and credit markets.

The capital markets use TBA prices in order to determine the *current coupon* or the *secondary mortgage rate*. This rate is the basis for setting the *primary mortgage rate* that is offered to retail customers. The current coupon $\mathfrak{M}(t)$ for a given settlement T_0 is defined as the coupon C on a TBA which settles on T_0 and whose value is par. In practice, such TBAs rarely exit, but they can be created synthetically. Namely, for settlements not exceeding the longest traded PSA date, one can interpolate the coupons and settlement dates. For settlement dates past the longest traded PSA date, we model the TBA prices based on the currently calibrated term structure and prepayment models. Then, from the TBA valuation formula,

$$\mathfrak{M}(t) = \frac{1 - \mathrm{PO}(t)}{\mathfrak{A}(t)} .$$

As a consequence, $\mathfrak{M}(t)$ is a tradeable asset, if the amortizing annuity is used as a numeraire, and its dynamics is given by a martingale.

The mortgage measure is useful in the definition of the *constant maturity mortgage* (CMM) rate, which enters forward rate agreements on future values of the mortgage rate. Such contracts, and their multiperiod versions, are traded in the US dollar market. The rates on these contracts are defined in analogy with the CMS rate and CMDS spread. Namely, the CMM rate is given by

$$\mathrm{CMM}(T_{0:m}; T^p) = \mathsf{E}^{\mathsf{Q}_{T^p}} [\mathfrak{M}(T_{0:m})] , \tag{129}$$

where Q_{T^p} is the forward measure associated with the payment date on the contract. Arguing as in the cases of CMS and CMDS, we can express the CMM rate in terms of the (forward) current coupon rate and a convexity adjustment.

MBS markets are very complex, and we have focused only on their most liquid sector. Instruments collateralized by other types of loans, such as loans with terms shorter than thirty years, or loans with adjustable rates, are also traded. Non-agency instruments, which are collateralized by nonconforming loans, pose a modeling challenge, as they exhibit complex credit risk in addition to the prepayment risk. All aspects of these markets is discussed thoroughly in [8] and [6].

References

[1] Andersen, L. Lecture Notes on Credit Models, Courant Institute of Mathematical Sciences (2009).

[2] Björk,T. *Arbitrage Theory in Continuous Time*, Oxford University Press (2009).

[3] Blanchet-Scalliet, C., El Karoui, N., and Martellini, L. Dynamic asset pricing theory with uncertain time-horizon, *J. Econ. Dyn. Contr.*, **29**, 1737–1764 (2005).

[4] Brigo, D. Multi-currency credit default swaps, *Int. J. Theor. Appl. Finance*, **22**, 1950018 (2019).

[5] Brigo, D., and Mercurio, F. *Interest Rate Models: Theory and Practice*, Springer Verlag (2006).

[6] Davidson, A., and Levin, A. *Mortgage Valuation Models*, Oxford University Press (2014).

[7] Dehm, J. C. *Stochastic Mortality: Modeling and Optimal Investment*, University of Ulm (2020).

[8] Fabozzi, F. J. *The Handbook of Mortgage-Backed Securities*, Oxford University Press (2016).

[9] Felpel, M., Kienitz, J., and McWalter, T. A. Effective stochastic volatility: applications to ZABR-type models, *Quantitative Finance*, **21**, 837–852 (2021).

[10] Geman, H., El Karoui, N., and Rochet, J.-C. Changes of numeraire, changes of probability measure and option pricing, *J. Appl. Prob.*, **32**, 443–458 (1995).

[11] Hagan, P. CMS conundrums: pricing CMS swaps, caps, and floors, *Wilmott Magazine*, **March**, 38–44 (2004).

[12] Hagan, P. S., Kumar, D., Lesniewski, A., and Woodward, D. E. Managing smile risk, *Wilmott Magazine*, **September**, 84–108 (2002).

[13] Hagan, P. S., and Lesniewski, A. LIBOR market model with SABR style stochastic volatility, preprint (2008).

[14] Hagan, P. S., Lesniewski, A., Skoufis, G. E., and Woodward, D. E. Convexity without replication, *Wilmott Magazine*, **January**, 58–69 (2020).

[15] Harrison, J. M., and Kreps, and D. M. Martingales and arbitrage in multiperiod securities markets, *J. Econ. Theory*, **20**, 381–408 (1979).

[16] Harrison, J. M., and Pliska, S. R. Martingales and stochastic integrals in the theory of continuous trading, *Stoch. Proc. Appl.*, **11**, 215–260 (1981).

[17] Jamshidian, F. Valuation of credit default swaps and swaptions, *Finance and Stochastics*, **8**, 343–371 (2004).

[18] Lando, D., and Nielsen, A. B. Quanto CDS Spreads. SSRN 3268890 (2018).

[19] Lyashenko, A., and Mercurio, F. Looking forward to backward-looking rates: completing the generalized forward market model, preprint (2021).

[20] Musiela, M., and Rutkowski, M. *Martingale Methods in Financial Modeling*, Springer Verlag (2004).

[21] Oksendal, B. *Stochastic Differential Equations: An Introduction with Applications*, Springer Verlag (2013).

[22] Pelsser, A. Mathematical foundation of convexity correction, *Quant. Finance*, **3**, 59–65 (2003).

[23] Rebonato, R. *Modern Pricing of Interest-Rate Derivatives: The LIBOR Market Model and Beyond*, Princeton University Press (2002).

[24] Rebonato, R., McKay, K., and White, R. *The SABR/LIBOR Market Model: Pricing, Calibration and Hedging for Complex Interest-Rate Derivatives*, Wiley (2009).

[25] Rudin, W. *Real and Complex Analysis*, McGraw Hill (1986).

[26] Schönbucher, P. A note on survival measures and the pricing of options on credit default swaps, working paper (2003).

[27] Schweizer, M. A guided tour through quadratic hedging approaches, SFB 373 discussion paper (1991).

[28] Turfus, C. Analytic pricing of quanto CDS, researchgate.net (2019).

Acknowledgment

We would like to thank Riccardo Rebonato for his invitation to contribute to the Elements in Quantitative Finance series.

Cambridge Elements

Quantitative Finance

Riccardo Rebonato
EDHEC Business School

Editor Riccardo Rebonato is Professor of Finance at EDHEC Business School and holds the PIMCO Research Chair for the EDHEC Risk Institute. He has previously held academic positions at Imperial College, London, and Oxford University, and has been Global Head of Fixed Income and FX Analytics at PIMCO, and Head of Research, Risk Management and Derivatives Trading at several major international banks. He has previously been on the Board of Directors for ISDA and GARP, and he is currently on the Board of the Nine Dot Prize. He is the author of several books and articles in finance and risk management, including *Bond Pricing and Yield Curve Modelling* (2017, Cambridge University Press).

About the Series

Cambridge Elements in Quantitative Finance aims for broad coverage of all major topics within the field. Written at a level appropriate for advanced undergraduate or graduate students and practitioners, *Elements* combines reports on original research covering an author's personal area of expertise, tutorials and masterclasses on emerging methodologies, and reviews of the most important literature.

Cambridge Elements

Quantitative Finance

Elements in the Series

Machine Learning for Asset Managers
Marcos M. López de Prado

Advances in Retirement Investing
Lionel Martellini and Vincent Milhau

A Practitioner's Guide to Discrete-Time Yield Curve Modelling: With Empirical Illustrations and MATLAB Examples
Ken Nyholm

Girsanov, Numeraires, and All That
Patrick S. Hagan and Andrew Lesniewski

A full series listing is available at: www.cambridge.org/EQF

Printed in the United States
by Baker & Taylor Publisher Services